Shared Mission
Religious Education in the Catholic Tradition

Leonardo Franchi

SHARED MISSION:
RELIGIOUS EDUCATION
IN THE CATHOLIC TRADITION

Scepter
London

This edition of *Shared Mission: Religious Education in the Catholic Tradition* is published in England by Scepter (U.K.) Ltd., 21 Hinton Avenue, Hounslow TW4 6AP; e-mail: scepter@pobox.com

ISBN-13: 978-1-910644-07-2

© This edition – Scepter (U.K.) Ltd., 2016

Cover design, text revision and typeset by KW Intermedia, and printed in the EU.

CONTENTS

PREFACE

This volume on the relationship between catechesis and Religious Education is a timely reminder of the importance of authentic Catholic Education. As the Church of the New Evangelisation, we need increasingly to deepen our engagement with the many traditions and practices revealed in Sacred Tradition. Catholic Religious Education should help us to do this.

Our Catholic educational heritage is a gift to humanity, not just a private tradition to be cherished by the baptised. Where would contemporary education be without the influence of the early monastic communities, the cathedral schools and the reforming energy of Charlemagne and Alcuin of York? How fortunate we are to have St. Ignatius of Loyola, St. John Baptiste de La Salle, St. John Bosco and Maria Montessori in our pantheon of educational reformers!

In Catholic schools, Religious Education must be grounded in Catholic theology. Wider educational theory has much to contribute to human flourishing but Catholic schools are the site of a sincere dialogue between such ideas and the principles of Catholic theology. To be a Catholic educator is to seek harmony between faith and reason, theory and practice: such a dialogue is a *sine qua non* of an excellent Catholic school. As the Congregation for Catholic Education has recently reminded us, contemporary Catholic schools are called to be sites of intercultural dialogue.[1] This dialogue should be sincere, rooted in tradition and open to fresh thinking.

Catholic Education, however, must have a commitment to the formation of the baptised. The wider catechetical processes of the Church are not left at the door of the

---

[1] Congregation for Catholic Education, *Educating to Intercultural Dialogue in Catholic Schools: Living in Harmony for a Civilization of Love*, 2013

Catholic school but are reshaped and applied to the life and context of a pluralistic educational body. The Religious Education curriculum contributes to the faith formation of the baptised by presenting the Sacred Tradition in an accessible and systematic way. Religious Education hence provides a worthy architecture for the life of Catholic schools. Let there be no doubt: it is not possible to have an effective and successful Catholic school if it fails in its provision of Religious Education.

In presenting the argument for *communio* as the ideal paradigm for developing the relationship between catechesis and Religious Education, this book offers the contemporary Church a theologically refined set of proposals to serve the New Evangelisation in Catholic schools. In my address to delegates gathered at the University of Glasgow for the launch of the St Andrew's Foundation for Catholic Teacher Education in 2013, I mentioned the importance of *communio* in the life of the Church:

> Communion comes about through initial conversion to the person of Christ and necessarily leads to communion with everything with which Christ is in communion.

This is the task that lies ahead. I ask all with an interest in the Catholic educational project to consider seriously the issues raised in this important volume.

Gerhard Cardinal Müller
Prefect
Congregation for the Doctrine of the Faith
Rome, 14 July 2016

AUTHOR'S PROLOGUE

This book is a contribution to scholarship in the field of Religious Education. [1] My aim is simple: to offer a critical perspective on the nature of Religious Education in the light of contemporary developments in Catholic thinking in catechesis and wider thinking in education. It is my hope that the issues raised herein will provide ample material for fruitful dialogue and constructive debate in the world of Catholic Education.

I am pleased to acknowledge my scholarly debt to giants in the field. From the calendar of saints, I drew happily, and with much fruit, on the work of the following: St Augustine of Hippo, St Thomas Aquinas, St Ignatius of Loyola and St John Baptiste de la Salle. I am equally in the debt of those who have contributed so much to recent scholarship: Josef Jungmann, Eugene Kevane, Thomas Groome, Richard Rymarz, Graeme Rossiter, Jim Conroy, Bob Davies and Stephen McKinney. To Bob and Stephen, a special 'thank you' for your advice, encouragement and support during the preparation of this text. I also extend my gratitude to Professor Richard Rymarz for his endorsement. This was especially pleasing given his status as a world class scholar in the field.

I am especially grateful to Cardinal Gerhard Müller, Prefect of the Congregation for the Doctrine of the Faith for agreeing to write the Preface to this book. I am honoured and humbled by this generous gesture.

Leonardo Franchi
15 August 2016

---

[1] I will initial captials for Religious Education throughout the text as it refers to a distinct curricular subject.

Santa Maria, Spes Nostra, Sedes Sapientiae, Ora pro Nobis

INTRODUCTION

This work examines the relationship between catechesis and school-based Religious Education as expressed in the Catholic educational tradition. [1] It offers a rationale for contemporary Religious Education which is rooted in Catholic theology while informed by solid pedagogical foundations.

The distinctive yet complementary relationship between catechesis and Religious Education is an important theme in contemporary Catholic educational thought. A firm and nuanced understanding of the nature of this important relationship and its historical roots is essential to an authentic understanding of both fields of study.

It should not be a surprise that the conceptual framework of Religious Education is complex and multi-layered. In essence, it can be boiled down to the following question: To what extent can the curricular subject of Religious Education be the primary vehicle for the faith formation of pupils in the Catholic school? When posed in these terms, are there possible lines of tension between *one* Religious Education curriculum offered both to pupils from Catholic families and to those who belong to other religious and philosophical traditions? Furthermore, is there a wider cultural issue regarding the role of religion in a pluralist educational

---

[1] Henceforth the term Religious Education refers to a subject in the curriculum of the Catholic school – unless expressly stated otherwise.

environment? Both questions inform the ideas presented in this volume.

A healthy relationship between catechesis and Religious Education offers rich possibilities for a renewed vision for Catholic Education. An authentically Catholic curriculum in Religious Education needs to be both grounded in Tradition and outward-facing. All pupils are invited to engage meaningfully with the tenets of Catholic thought, and to respond appropriately.

Given this high level of expectation, and in order to present a suitable way forward for policy-makers and all with an interest in Catholic Education, I offer three arguments to underpin a refreshed vision of Religious Education in the contemporary Catholic school:

- The relationship between catechesis and Religious Education is most fully understood in broader historical and theological contexts. We need to draw from our traditions in order to move forward;
- The theology of ecclesial communion (*communio*) offers a suitable framework within which the partnership between catechesis and Religious Education can be developed. This offers subtlety and balance to an issue which lies at the heart of the Catholic school's self-understanding and its relationship to wider society;
- Religious Education is a dynamic partnership between principles of catechesis and principles of Catholic Education. A harmonious interplay of concepts is mutually beneficial.

Addressing these claims allows us to go on an interesting journey through selected aspects of Catholic theology and the history of education. This scholarly adventure, so to speak, will shed some light on contemporary developments in Church teaching and practice in schools.

We are currently living in the era of the New

Evangelisation.[2] There is much to be done to reclaim the intellectual foundations of Catholic Education which have been so disturbed by the advances of secularism in its many subtle yet influential guises. Religious Education curricula in Catholic schools, regrettably, have not been immune to the influence of such ideologies.

Given the important role of the Catholic school in the life of the Church, the time is ripe for a fresh study of how the Religious Education curriculum can make an effective and lasting contribution to developing the Church's mission in the era of the New Evangelisation. As Religious Education provides much of the intellectual and pastoral energy underpinning the wider life of the contemporary Catholic school, it is self-evident that the Church needs to look again at how this much contested subject area can be developed in line with authentic Catholic tradition.[3]

The later years of the 20th century and early years of the 21st century was a period rich in teachings from the Magisterium of the Catholic Church on the topics of catechesis and Catholic Education. The publication of three major Church documents on catechesis underlined its importance to the contemporary Church.[4] During the same period, the Magisterium published some important, if underused, documents on Catholic Education.[5] Much of this corpus remains hidden

---

[2] The *Pontifical Council for the Promoting of the New Evangelisation*, a dicastery of the Roman Curia, is responsible for overseeing all matters related to the New Evangelisation. See also Pope Benedict XVI, *Apostolic Letter 'Motu Propri Data' Ubicumque et Semper,* (2010), which established this organ of the Holy See.

[3] The use of 'contested' here is important: it refers to the fact that many voices in education refuse to accept that Religious Education and 'faith' (broadly understood) have any place in the school curriculum. See, for example, L. Franchi, J. Conroy and S. McKinney, 'Religious Education'. In D. Wyse, L. Hayward and J. Pandya (Eds.) *The SAGE Handbook of Curriculum, Pedagogy and Assessment.* (London: Sage Publications, 2015).

[4] Congregation for the Clergy, *General Catechetical Directory,* 1971; Pope John Paul II, *Catechesi Tradendae,* 1979; *General Directory for Catechesis,* 1997.

[5] Congregation for Catholic Education, *The Catholic School,* 1977; *Lay Catholics in Schools: Witnesses to Faith,* 1982; *The Religious Dimension of Education in a*

from those charged with leading Catholic schools at a local level. It is my contention in the present volume that a desire to engage meaningfully with this body of work is a *sine qua non* of effective and fruitful Catholic Education.

Regarding the distinction between catechesis and Religious Education, it is essential that we do not misconstrue what is proposed here. While 'distinction' is a powerful term, it does not here connote stark difference but an evolving relationship in which each category is able to speak to and with the other. Nonetheless, to ignore the distinction would be to indulge in a 'category mistake', the consequence of which could be the development of Religious Education programmes which are neither academically sound nor theologically robust.[6]

To be clear, catechesis is the parent of Religious Education. Religious Education is, hence, a *legitimate development* of the content and methods of effective catechesis.[7] As it is difficult to grasp fully the implications of the aforementioned distinction without a clear understanding of the genealogy of Catholic thinking on both topics, it is necessary to explore the shifting conceptual frameworks of Religious Education through two lenses: the history of catechesis and aspects of contemporary theological, catechetical and educational thought. This fertile and fluid framework reminds us that we are dealing with a debate rooted in the Catholic Church's distinguished

---

Catholic School, 1988; *The Catholic School on the Threshold of the Third Millennium*, 1997; *Educating Together in Catholic Schools: A Shared Mission between Consecrated Persons and the Lay Faithful*, 2007; *Circular Letter to Presidents of Bishops' Conferences on Religious Education in Schools*, 2009 and *Educating to Intercultural Dialogue in Catholic Schools: Living in Harmony for a Civilization of Love*, 2013.

[6] B. Hyde, A Category Mistake: Why Contemporary Australian Religious Education may be Doomed to Failure. *Journal of Beliefs and Values: Studies in Religion and Education*, 34 (1), 2013, pp. 36-45.

[7] For a brief overview of the challenges arising from drawing a sharp distinction between catechesis and Religious Education, see J. Fleming, Is There Anything Religious about Religious Education Any More? In M. Felderhof, P. Thomson and D. Torevell (Eds.), *Inspiring Faith in School: Studies in Religious Education*. (Aldershot: Ashgate, 2007).

theological and educational traditions.

To be clear, the present volume is neither a general history of education nor a history of Catholic Education. The focus is on the evolution of specific religious and educational ideas in the Catholic tradition. Nonetheless, wider frames of reference, notably the contribution of theological investigation to developments in catechesis and Religious Education, influence much of the debate.

Exploring Key Terms

It is important to explore three key terms in the subject-matter of the present book: *Catholic Education; Catechesis* and *Religious Education*. What follows is not a list of fixed definitions as such but initial ideas about the conceptual borders of the fields in question.

Catholic Education

The term 'Catholic Education' describes the totality of experiences, instruction, formation and support which the Church employs in order to foster the growth in virtue and wisdom of the human person.[8] Catholic Education is expressed principally in a network of primary, secondary and tertiary institutions which are governed by an educational philosophy which flows from considered reflection on Catholic doctrine.[9] The philosophy of Catholic Education is rooted in a specific anthropology: the human person is created in the image and likeness of God (*imago dei*) and yet is subject to the effects of Original Sin.[10] The human person is in turn "loved by God,

---

[8] See J. Maritain, *Education at the Crossroads*. (New Haven: Yale University Press, 1961). Maritain's work offers a thoughtful philosophical basis for any study of contemporary Catholic educational thought. It is fair to say that the works of Maritain are not a staple of contemporary reading lists for prospective teachers.

[9] M. Morey, Education in a Catholic Framework. In J. Piderit, and M. Morey (Eds.) *Teaching the Tradition: Academic Themes in Academic Disciplines*. (Oxford: Oxford University, Press, 2012), pp. 397-416.

[10] Cf. *Catechism of the Catholic Church*, 356-361; T. Rausch, Catholic Anthropology. In Piderit and Morey (Eds.), 2012, pp. 31-45.

with a mission on earth and a destiny that is immortal."[11]

Catholic Education is more than an institutionalised or scholastically-conditioned version of catechesis. Its scope goes beyond the world of Religious Education.[12] Catholic Education claims to promote the integral formation of the whole person "by means of a systematic and critical assimilation of culture."[13]

Integral formation, as here employed, connotes a complete education of the human person: it is an application of the relationship between faith and reason to education. In Catholic Education there can be no separation between acquisition of knowledge and growth in virtue. It ought to promote an openness to discussion and critical examination of a range of religious and cultural ideas in the light of both faith and reason. This allows it to remain a valid and rigorous educational experience for those who do not belong to the Catholic, or any other, religious tradition.[14]

Catechesis

Catechesis is the term traditionally used to describe the ongoing faith formation of the baptised. This process aims to make explicit and fruitful the energy emanating from the initial conversion.[15]

Catechesis has been normally understood as an *echoing* (or handing down) of the traditions, beliefs and practices of the believing community. The catechetical focus in the early Church was on the oral tradition as a means of communicating the message of the Gospel.[16] Two broader questions follow: Is there value in retaining the emphasis on orality and to what

[11] *The Religious Dimension of Education in a Catholic School*, 1988, 76.
[12] Benedict XVI, *Letter to the Faithful of the Diocese of Rome on the Urgent Task of Educating Young People, 2008.*
[13] *The Catholic School*, 1977, 26.
[14] For a contemporary summary of some of the nuances of Catholic educational practices, see D. Clayton, *The Way of Beauty: Liturgy, Education and Inspiration for Family, School and College.* (Kettering: Angelico Press, 2015), Ch. 3.
[15] *General Directory for Catechesis*, 1997. See in particular paragraph 82.
[16] Cf. *Catechesi Tradendae* 1979; R. Bauckham, *Jesus and the Eyewitnesses: The Gospels as Eyewitness Testimony.* (Michigan: Eerdmans Publishing Co. 2006).

extent can Catechesis as a term be used as an overarching expression for faith development? [17]

Catechesis in practice can be divided into two broad pathways: first, the post-evangelisation faith formation process of those preparing to enter into full communion with the Church and second, the ongoing faith formation of the baptised members of the Church. While the former would normally operate within the framework of the *Rite of Christian Initiation of Adults* (RCIA), the latter can assume many different forms: homilies during Church services or specific classes on a particular theme, for example, marriage. It also offers possibilities for more structured courses, possibly certificated, within the wider community of the Church. Whatever the context, pivotal to catechesis are the following: a) the assumption that faith in and intimacy with Christ is present; b) faith is developed and deepened in an atmosphere of ecclesial harmony and c) the connection between faith formation and the liturgy is made explicit as all catechesis has full participation, properly understood, in the liturgy as its objective. [18] This liturgical aspect is particularly prominent in the RCIA process which culminates in the reception of the candidate into full communion with the Catholic Church at the Easter Vigil Mass.

The Catechetical Movement of the early 20th Century sought to re-energise Catechesis in the light of scholarship in both theology and education. In the years following the Second Vatican Council (1962-1965), catechesis was gradually reconfigured to refer more to the life-long faith journey of the Christian person as opposed to a term describing the approach taken in the Religious Education class in the Catholic school.

---

[17] Cf. T. Groome, *Christian Religious Education: Sharing Our Story and Vision.* (San Francisco: Harper and Row, 1980); Total Catechesis/Religious Education: A Vision for Now and Always. In T. Groome, and H. Horell (Eds), *Horizons and Hopes: The Future of Religious Education.* (New Jersey: Paulist Press, 2003); P. Devitt, *That You May Believe: A Brief History of Religious Education.* (Dublin: Dominican Publications, 1992); L. Kelly, *Catechesis Revisited: Handing on the Faith Today.* (London: Darton Longman, 2000).
[18] Second Vatican Council, *Sacrosanctum Concilium,* 1964, 11.

This broader vision of the scope and purpose of catechesis prompted further discussion on whether the Catholic school was a suitable locus for a model of Religious Education underpinned by a predominantly catechetical framework.

Religious Education

The definition of Religious Education in the Magisterial corpus tends to be opaque. It remains a contested term both within and beyond the Christian traditions. In broad terms, conceptual frameworks of Religious Education are stretched along a continuum of meaning: at one end, it is closely related to, or co-terminus with, all forms of faith nurture, in other words, catechesis; at the other end of the spectrum, Religious Education is a non-confessional study of religious ways of understanding the world, dealing with the intersection of religion and education. A fuller analysis of this debate is found in Part Two.

A further distinction within the Catholic tradition is reflected in the present book's use of the terms *catechetical paradigm* and *educational paradigm* as descriptors of two conceptual frameworks of Religious Education. The former refers to models of Religious Education which draw heavily on catechetical principles; the latter refers to models of Religious Education which are strongly influenced by educational principles. This distinction, however, like so much in Catholic thought, lends itself to many subtle layers of nuance.

We must bear in mind, however, that we are exploring the contours of a curricular subject in a *Catholic* school. As such, it is helpful to show at this stage how the 'continuum of meaning' noted above has been articulated in statements on the purpose of Religious Education issued by different educational agencies of the Church.

One brief example illustrates the degree of conceptual confusion which had a significant, and not always helpful, impact on the shape of the subject. In 1986, the Catholic Bishops' Conference of England and Wales issued guidelines for Religious Education (*Statement on Religious Education in*

Schools) which reflected a model of Religious Education understood broadly as a study of religions and religious ways of
thinking.[19] According to this document, "Religious education
is *not primarily* concerned with maturing and developing
Christian faith. Its aim is to help people to be aware of and
appreciate the religious dimension of life and the way this has
been expressed in religious traditions."

By way of contrast, the syllabus for Scottish Catholic
Schools, *This Is Our Faith* (published in 2011), pushed the
meaning of Religious Education very close to established
definitions of the related term, catechesis. *This Is Our Faith*
defines Religious Education in Catholic schools as a process
which both offers opportunities for evangelisation and
catechesis – here defined as "the deepening of existing faith
commitments among believers." [20]

It needs to be borne in mind that these statements come
from documents which are separated by a period of twenty-
five years. During this time, the Church's position on the
primary purpose of Religious Education underwent substantial
modification, as we will see. Nonetheless, the divergence in
thought is striking. This juxtaposition serves as a thematic
signpost to the issues at the heart of the present book.

Overview of the Book

Part One revolves around four historical contexts selected
specifically to illuminate contemporary developments in the
field. While these historical periods have porous boundaries,
they offer a working structure in support of the core claims of
the book. The development of Catholic teaching on catechesis
and Religious Education is an example of the interaction of
change and continuity: each historical period, in response to
evolving social, cultural and political milieux, reshapes the
tradition it has inherited. While this book does not claim to
offer a global evaluation of the educational, theological and

---

[19] J. Gallagher, *Living and Sharing Our Faith: National Project of Catechesis and Religious Education.* (London: Collins Liturgical Publications, 1986).
[20] Scottish Catholic Education Service, *This is Our Faith.* (Glasgow, 2011).

political arguments of the selected periods, the aftershocks of these debates remain pertinent to the configuration of catechesis and Religious Education today.

Part Two explores the complex genealogy of the relationship between catechesis and Religious Education. Key thematic frames of reference within which the relevant Magisterial documents and associated academic literature are set out and explored chronologically thus allowing for some cross-referencing across the themes: unsurprisingly the range of the issues for debate resists a neat packaging within specific time-frames but does provide a helpful working structure. The four chapters of Part Two will demonstrate that the initial thematic interplay between the academic literature (secondary sources) and the Magisterial documents (primary sources) led in time to the clear articulation of the distinction between catechesis and Religious Education in the Magisterial documents.

Part Three proposes that a Spirituality of Communion should underpin the Church's work in catechesis, education and Religious Education. To do this requires mature reflection on aspects of the theology of *communio* and consideration of its implications for the Church's many formational initiatives. The term 'Shared Mission' is introduced as a way to find a harmonious relationship between catechesis and Religious Education. Shared Mission seems to be a satisfactory articulation of the necessary dialogic relationship between both fields and offers a suitable space for both distinction and reciprocity.

PART ONE
MODELS OF RELIGIOUS FORMATION:
FOUR HISTORICAL CONTEXTS

How appropriate is it to view the life of the Church at certain periods of history as normative for future generations? If we were to fall into the trap of revering the past as somehow purer and more pristine than the present, Christian belief and practice would remain rooted in what was believed and practised at particular points in time and hence restrict theology and any form of Christian studies to the purely historical forensic domain.[1] Of course, this does not lessen the value of historical study. Far from it. It simply locates it in a wider and more fluid framework.

Any historical study of catechetical and educational developments must take into account the relevant social and cultural contexts in which they emerged. For example, mass education, as commonly understood today, would be a concept unknown to those who lived before the nineteenth century. The limited involvement of 'the child' in education and the nature of children's place in society at this time militate against drawing exact parallels between particular points in history and contemporary attitudes to education and schooling.[2]

---

[1] H. Jedin, General Introduction to Church History. In H. Jedin and J. Dolan (Eds.), *History of the Church Vol. 1: From the Apostolic Community to Constantine.* (London: Burns and Oates, 1980).

[2] For more on the place of the child in society, see the following studies:

Evidence from the selected historical periods suggests strongly the predominance of the *catechetical paradigm* (see Introduction) firmly rooted in the theological and cultural resources of Catholic Christianity. Alongside this, an *educational paradigm* gradually evolved in response to the Church's dialogue with wider thinking. To demonstrate the fluid nature of the relationship, four selected historical contexts offer important indicators of the parameters of religious formation in the Church. This offers glimpses of an evolving relationship which has culminated in the contemporary distinction between catechesis and Religious Education. The four selected contexts are:

- Catechesis in the Apostolic and Patristic Ages (Ch. 1);
- Catechesis in the Middle Ages (Ch. 2);
- The Catholic Reform and Catechesis (Ch. 3);
- The Catechetical Renewal of the Early Twentieth Century (Ch. 4).

M. Bunge (Ed.), *The Child in Christian Thought.* (Cambridge: Eerdmans Publishing Company, 2001); O.M. Bakke, *When Children Became People: The Birth of Childhood in Early Christianity.* (Minneapolis: Fortress Press, 2005). (Translated by B. McNeil.); C. Horn and J. Martens, *'Let the Little Children Come to Me': Childhood and Children in Early Christianity.* (Washington DC: Catholic University of America Press, 2009).

CHAPTER 1
CATECHESIS IN THE APOSTOLIC AND PATRISTIC AGES

Catechesis in the Apostolic and Patristic Ages, the first historical context, covers the period from Apostolic times until the time of St Augustine of Hippo (AD 354-430). As St Augustine's writings on catechesis and educational matters form the first cohesive 'philosophy' of Christian education, it is reasonable to posit his life and work as a key pivot in the development of broader Christian educational ideas.[1]

If it is accepted that Christian doctrine and practice develop over the ages, the study of the life of the early Church offers valuable insights into the emerging Christian community's self-understanding and praxis.[2]

Owing to the paucity of relevant primary texts on the question of children's religious formation in the period available to us, an element of selection is inevitable. These texts have to be read in the context of the wider patristic corpus where

---

[1] Cf. E. Kevane, *Augustine the Educator: A Study in the Fundamentals of Christian Formation.* (Westminster, Maryland: The Newman Press, 1964); R. Topping, *Happiness and Wisdom: Augustine's Early Theology of Education.* (Washington DC: Catholic University of America Press, 2012).

[2] Cf. JH. Newman, *An Essay on the Development of Christian Doctrine.* (Notre Dame, Indiana: University of Notre Dame Press, 1878/2003), chs. 2 and 3: G. Evans, Introduction. In G. Evans, *The First Christian Theologians.* (Oxford: Blackwell Publishing, 2005).

the writings of the Church Fathers are examples of a perceived theological freshness and energy. In this light, the catechetical paradigm of early Christian education as here presented had three distinct and interrelated themes.

Theme 1: The Moral and Pastoral Formation of the Child in Early Christianity

For the first Christians, the key educational question was one of evangelisation: how to pass on their faith in the risen Jesus to those around them in response to the 'great commission' of Matthew 28:19-20 [3] Indeed, all Christian thinking on education is rooted in and developed from this call to evangelise.[4]

The extant Christian writings from the first five centuries refer in broad terms to the question of children's human and religious formation.[5] They do not offer precise and practical details of this process beyond the restating of the direct responsibility of parents to rear their children in good living.[6] The lack of evidence as such is not insignificant; it shows that in early Christianity, catechesis was part of the home-centred nurturing of the child and the clear responsibility of the blood-family, assisted by the wider community of believers. The contemporary understanding of Christian education as a process involving a range of dedicated establishments would have been unrecognisable to the early Church.

---

[3] "Go therefore and make disciples of all nations, baptising them in the name of the Father and of the Son and of the Holy Spirit, teaching them to observe all that I have commanded you: and lo, I am with you always, to the close of the age" (New Testament, Revised Standard Version).

[4] *Circular Letter to Presidents of Bishops' Conferences on Religious Education in Schools*, 2009.

[5] J. Marmion, *Catholic Traditions in Education*. (Macclesfield: St Edward's Press, 1986).

[6] St John Chrysostom (347-407 AD) is an invaluable primary source for early Christianity's approach to the rearing of children. See St John Chrysostom, Address on Vainglory and the Right Way for Parents to Bring Up Their Children. In M. Laistner, *Christianity and Pagan Culture in the Later Roman Empire*. (New York: Cornell University Press, 1967).

There is a congruence between the Jewish notion of children's religious formation and the approach adopted in the early Church. What they have in common is a set of processes centred on the home and the synagogue/Christian community with no division between the notion of education and religious learning.[7] The Jewish school system, as organised in the first century, was a way of maintaining religious and cultural identity in the face of the perceived attractions of Greek philosophy.[8] It is reasonable to suggest that the children of the first Jewish converts to Christianity continued to attend these schools and received supplementary instruction on the Christian Gospel at other times. This would align with the broader evidence that the early Christians of Jerusalem continued to adhere to their inherited forms of piety by attending Temple worship before coming to 'break bread' in their homes.[9]

The Gospel evidence on the place of children in the early Church community is scant but clear. Any discussion of the representation of children in the New Testament needs, of course, to be aware of both figurative and literal uses of the term in the texts. Nonetheless, children are included in the groups of people who heard Jesus preach;[10] they are held up as models of humility[11] and were included, it seems, in the first missionary journeys.[12] Similarly, in the writings of St Paul there is evidence of the importance placed on the family's responsibility for the faith-formation of the young.[13] While the term 'children' is clearly used in the Gospels in a figurative sense,[14] there was little recognition of the need to have specific

---

[7] Cf. Book of Deuteronomy 4:9; J. Grundy Volf, The Least and the Greatest: Children in the New Testament. In M. Bunge (Ed.) *The Child in Christian Thought*, 2001.

[8] W. Strange, *Children in the Early Church*. (Milton Keynes: Paternoster, 2006).

[9] *Acts of the Apostles* 2:46.

[10] Cf. *John* 6:9 and *Matthew* 14:21.

[11] *Matthew* 18-1-3.

[12] *Acts* 21:1-6.

[13] cf. *Colossians* 3:20-21; *Ephesians* 6:1-4.

[14] *Mark* 9:36-37.

processes for children's catechesis.[15] This is not necessarily evidence of neglect of children's religious formations: on the contrary, children in the Gospel are normally depicted as models of fidelity and receptiveness to the message of Jesus.[16]

By the late first century the inherited (from Judaism) faith-nurture approach to education had, unsurprisingly, developed a distinct Christian flavour.[17] This approach was pastoral in nature and characterised by eager impulses to foster faith in the context of the liturgical life of the believing community. It was a Christian interpretation of the Greek concept of *paideia*.[18] This is an early and important example of the *catechetical paradigm* of Religious Education in action, so to speak.

By the late 4th century, it is possible to speak of an emerging Christian pastoral theology for children.[19] A key figure in this development, St John Chrysostom (347-407), argued that the raising of the child in virtue was the true end of parenthood and education.[20] As Jewish education required study of the Torah, so St John Chrysostom placed the study of the Christian Scriptures at the heart of the educational process.

What makes St John Chrysostom's intervention crucial is that he encouraged the father of the family to use *story* as a medium to inculcate virtue in the child and, significantly,

---

[15] C. Horn and J. Martens, *'Let the Little Children Come to Me': Childhood and Children in Early Christianity,* 2009.

[16] cf: *Matthew* 18:1-5; 19:14-15

[17] cf. I. Clement chapter 1; Polycarp's Letter to the Philippians; Didache. In A. Louth and M. Staniforth (Eds.), *Early Christian Writings.* (London: Penguin, 1987).

[18] For more on Catechesis in this period, see: W. Jaegger, *Early Christianity and Greek Paideia.* (Cambridge: Belknap Press of Harvard University Press, 1961/1977) and R. Feldmeier, Before the Teachers of Israel and the Sages of Greece: Luke-Acts as a Precursor of the Conjunction of Biblical Faith and Hellenistic Education. In I. Tanaseanu-Doble and M. Dobler, (Eds.) *Religious Education in Pre Modern Europe.* (Boston: Brill, 2012), pp. 77-95.

[19] V. Guroian, The Ecclesial Family. In M. Bunge (Ed.)*The Child in Christian Thought,* 2001.

[20] St John Chrysostom, Address on *Vainglory and the Right Way for Parents to bring up their Children,* para. 19f.

suggested the adaptation of Gospel passages to the age and intellectual capability of the listener.[21] The focus here on educational method is a modest sign of a growing Christian engagement with the human person's developmental needs in the matter of religious formation. It is a notable episode in the Christian community's attempts to develop its range of suitable educational methods. St John Chrysostom's contribution is an indication of an emerging *educational paradigm* which moves within and is supportive of the predominant *catechetical paradigm.*

Such considered focus on the methods required to promote the moral and pastoral formation of young Christians was set alongside their sacramental needs. This leads to the second theme of the development of the *catechetical paradigm.*

Theme 2: The Child and the Sacramental Life of the Christian Community

There is little to suggest that the first Christians employed catechetical processes or strategies tailored specifically to the needs of children. Indeed, the lack of concrete historical evidence on the method and content of children's catechesis implies that the Church continued to view the formation of children primarily as a matter for the family assisted by the wider Church community. The liturgy would have acted as a living curriculum through which Christian doctrine would have been taught: the Church as a worshipping community was also the Church as a catechetical community. Such liturgically-focussed methods, for example, allowed children to play a full part as *lectors* (readers) and singers in choir.[22] The

---

[21] Is it possible that St John Chrysostom was aware of and sought to apply St Basil the Great's (330-379) four *principles* of reading Christian poetry? These principles are: the hermeneutical principle; the principle of selective reading; the principle of moral development and the principle of precaution. See A. Schwab, From a Way of Reading to a Way of Life: Basil of Caesarea and Gregory of Nazianus about Poetry in Christian Education. In *Religious Education in Pre Modern Europe*, 2012, pp. 147-162.

[22] Cf. Bakke, *When Children Became People: The Birth of Childhood in Early Christianity.* 2005, pp.225f and Horn and Martens, *'Let the Little Children Come*

debates over the desirability of infant baptism, alongside the rise of the catechumenate offer further examples of the Christian community's broadening of the processes of Christian formation and reflect a modest strengthening of the *catechetical paradigm.*

Regarding the practice of Infant Baptism, it is hard to ascertain the exact date of its origin. The New Testament tells us clearly that many households were baptised, thus suggesting strongly that children were included.[23] Later accounts of the development of the catechumenate and the Easter Vigil ceremonies in the late 2nd/early 3rd century state that children were baptised during the Easter Vigil along with their parents or another member of the extended family who would answer the priest's questions on the child's behalf.[24]

As the Church expanded throughout the Mediterranean basin and beyond in the first two centuries, its approach to the religious formation of the community adapted to meet these new and challenging circumstances. The *catechumenate* was the Church's response to the challenges arising from increased numbers of adults who wanted to become Christian.[25] As the demand for the baptism of infants belonging to these families increased, adult baptism became the exception, and not the norm.

St Cyril of Jerusalem's (314-396) catechetical lectures in the 4th century reveal the catechumente to be a rigorous and intellectually demanding preparation for baptism.[26] While

---

to Me': Childhood and Children in Early Christianity, 2009, pp. 296-297.

[23] Cf. *Acts* 2:38; 16:15; 16:33 and 18:8.

[24] For a fascinating overview of this period, see: K. Baus, The Great Church of Early Christian Times (c. AD 180-324). In Jedin and Dolan (Eds.), *History of the Church Vol. 1: From the Apostolic Community to Constantine*, 1980, pp. 215-432. See also St Cyprian of Carthage, *To Fidus, On the Baptism of Infants* (Epistle 58:6); http://www.newadvent.org/fathers/050658.htm

[25] Broadly speaking, the catechumenate was a three year process of examination and instruction; it could be understood as a coming together of various catechetical/educational and ritual processes culminating in the sacrament of Baptism at the Easter Vigil ceremonies.

[26] St Cyril's catechetical lectures are available in E. Yarnold (Ed.), *Cyril of*

children and adults were baptised at these ceremonies, it is unclear from the available sources just how the catechumenate was adapted, if at all, to the varying needs of the children. As already noted, the paucity of available evidence suggests that the ongoing family, community and liturgical life of the Church was the sum of the catechetical processes for children.

In parallel with the growth of the Church, there emerged initial signs of a major development in attitudes towards other ways of thinking. The Church's encounter with Greek philosophy become foundational to its developing identity and had significant implications for its catechetical and educational actions.

Theme 3: The Emerging Philosophy of Christian Education
The encounter with Greek philosophy was the seed of Christianity's renowned partnership between faith and reason.

The early Christian Apologists were willing to engage in dialogue on theological and cultural issues.[27] Their *educational method* consisted of nothing more than a clearly structured presentation to their various interlocutors.[28] It is, however, the encounter of the doctrine of the risen Jesus with the intellectual apparatus of Greek thought which marks a key stage in the development of an *educational paradigm* of Religious Education as we understand it today. This is when a distinct philosophy of Christian education begins to emerge.

While a contemporary understanding of philosophy rests primarily on its identity as an academic discipline, the ancient Greeks saw it first and foremost as a way of living with knowledge understood as a path to virtue.[29] In this respect, the Greek

---

Jerusalem. (London: Routledge, 2000).
[27] St Irenaus of Lyon (130-202) and St Justin the Martyr (100-165) are the most famous of this group. St Justin the Martyr's important contribution to the emerging Christian education tradition can be appreciated in his dialogues:http://www.newadvent.org/cathen/08580c.htm For a richly contextualised overview of this period, see H. Chadwick, *Early Christian Thought and the Classical Traditions*. (Oxford: Oxford University Press, 1984).
[28] A. Dulles, *A History of Apologetics*. (San Francisco: Ignatius Press, 1999).
[29] P. Hadot, *Philosophy as a Way of Life*. (Oxford: Blackwell Publishing,

approach seemed to overlap with the Christian claim to truth. Indeed the New Testament actually records the initial encounters between followers of Christianity and the adherents of Greek philosophy.[30]

Within this shifting intellectual climate, the early catechetical schools – although more of a process than a physical building – became the focus of a profound cultural dialogue between Christian thinking and traditional Greek philosophy. These initially private undertakings offered an integration of religious values, philosophy and high moral standards.[31] There is, crucially, no sense of dissonance between what the present study has identified as the *educational* and *catechetical* paradigms of Religious Education. It is hard, however, to identify specific indicators of the *modus operandi* of these institutions and of their locus, if any, in the education of children.

The most famous of these schools was the *School of Alexandria*. This institution allowed many of the ruling classes in this important metropolis to attain a high degree of cultural awareness. It is not surprising that it played a pivotal role in the development of the conceptual framework of early Christian education. One of the leaders of this school, St Clement of Alexandria (150-215), argued that as God is the origin of all good things, the good fruits of Greek philosophy must originate in God.[32] For example, St Clement claimed that the study of Greek philosophy was a "preparatory training to those who attain to faith through demonstration."[33]

2008). (Translated by Michael Chase.) See also R. Topping, *Happiness and Wisdom: Augustine's Early Theology of Education*, 2012).

[30] cf. *Acts* 17:16-34

[31] See K. Baus, The Great Church of Early Christian Times, c. AD 180-324. In Jedin and Dolan (Eds.), *History of the Church Vol. 1: From the Apostolic Community to Constantine*, 1980.

[32] St Clement of Alexandria, *Stromata*, Book 1:7:19.

[33] St Clement of Alexandria, *Stromata*. In A. Roberts and J. Donaldson, (Eds.) *Ante-Nicene Library Translations of the Writings of the Fathers down to AD 325*. (Edinburgh: T and T Clark, 1867). Ch. V.

The dialogue between Christianity and Greek philosophy had implications for Christian thinking on catechesis. The work of St Augustine of Hippo (354-430) offers an early defining example of the fruit of the marriage between Christianity and Greek philosophy as applied to catechesis,[34] with glimpses therein of an emerging philosophy of Christian education.[35] His works in this field have strong claims to be among the first attempts to map out a meaningful rationale for Christian education.[36] This focus on the pedagogy of catechesis reflected the growing importance of an *educational paradigm* gradually influencing the now established *catechetical paradigm.*[37]

One of St Augustine's distinctive contributions to the catechetical/educational contours of the period lies principally in his work on the role of the Christian teacher. For Augustine, the teacher's role is to lead the student to the truth, understood as *knowledge* of Jesus.[38] St Augustine, drawing on Clement's *Paedagogus*, saw Jesus as the *Teacher* who teaches through the human teacher; it is the role of the (Christian) teacher hence to point towards this truth.[39]

---

[34] St Augustine of Hippo, *On the Catechizing of the Uninstructed.* (Whitefish: Kessinger Publishing Rare Reprints), Ch. 8.

[35] Cf. *De Magistro* – on the Teacher (AD 389). In King. P. (Ed.), *Against the Academicians* and *The Teacher.* (Indianapolis: Hackett Publishing Company, 1959); *De Catechezandi Rudibus – On the Catechizing of the Uninstructed* (AD 399). (Whitefish: Kessinger Publishing Rare Reprints.); *De Doctrina Christiana – On Christian Doctrine.* (AD 397-426), (Library of Liberal Arts, Indianapolis: Bobbs-Merrill Company, Inc., 1959. (Translated by D W Robertson.)

[36] Cf. E. Kevane, *Augustine the Educator: A Study in the Fundamentals of Christian Formation*, 1964, p. 124; C. Harrison, De Doctrina Christiana, *New Blackfriars* 87(1008), pp. 121-131; L. Franchi, St Augustine, Catechesis and Religious Education. *Religious Education* 106 (3), pp. 299-311 and Words are not Enough: The Teacher as Icon of the Truth in St Augustine. In R. McCluskey and S. McKinney (Eds.) *How the Teacher is Presented in Literature, History, Religion and the Arts: Cross-cultural Analyses of a Stereotype.* (Lampeter: Mellen Press, 2013).

[37] See O. Chadwick, *Augustine.* (Oxford: Oxford University Press, 1996) and M. Clark, *Augustine.* (London: Continuum, 2005) for accessible introductions to the life and thought of St Augustine of Hippo.

[38] St Augustine, The Teacher. In P. King (Ed.), 1995, 11:38.

[39] J. Drucker, Teaching as Pointing in 'The Teacher'. *Augustinian Studies* 1

While St John Chrysostom had recommended the use of story as a teaching medium with due adaptation for children, St Augustine promoted the use of the *narratio* in catechesis.[40] The *narratio*, the systematic mapping of the Christian story of salvation from Genesis to Christ, was a key teaching process in early Christianity. It embraced all catechumens in a Christocentric view of history in which all would be fulfilled in the world to come. The resultant teaching strategy, as set out by St Augustine, is a major, if understated, development in the philosophy of Christian education. It is an educational strategy designed to use the study of the 'wonderful facts' contained in Scripture as a way to enhance the catechetical processes in place.[41]

St Augustine presented Christian education as a process in which the sinner moves away from vice towards knowledge of Jesus and the practice of virtue. Both adults and children were, he claimed, in need of the grace given freely at Baptism to lead them away from sin and towards growth in virtue. While there is little in Augustine's wider corpus about adapting catechetical methodology to children, he advocated the adaptation of methodology to different groups of hearers.[42] The acceptance of the principle of differentiation offered the possibility of similar adaptation for children although this is not stated explicitly. The overall lack of concrete evidence of catechetical strategies for children once again suggests the continuation of the family and community-centred model of catechesis. There is the possibility of children being included

---

28, (2) 1997, pp. 101-132.

[40] For a critical exploration of St Augustine's perspectives on childhood, see M. Stortz, When Was Your Servant Innocent? Augustine on Childhood. In J. Bunge (Ed.), *The Child in Christian Thought*, 2001.

[41] Cf. St Augustine, *On the Catechizing of the Uninstructed* (Ch. 3) and *On Christian Doctrine*. IV.V. In contemporary language, such an approach offers *sacred history* as the curricular framework for the study of the Scriptures in the light of the divine pedagogy. See P. Willey, P. de Cointet and B. Morgan, *The Catechism of the Catholic Church and the Craft of Catechesis*. (San Francisco: Ignatius Press, 2008).

[42] St Augustine, *On the Catechizing of the Uninstructed*, Ch. 8 and Ch. 15.

in the wider catechetical processes involving the *narratio,* but this does not exclude the possibility of children attending some form of 'school'.

The three themes outlined above reveal, unsurprisingly, a Church determined to develop the faith of its adherents. The predominant *catechetical paradigm* is centred on integration into its sacramental and community life. There appears to have been little explicit recognition of the needs of children in this enterprise. The dialogue between Christianity and Greek philosophy did, however, make the Church more aware of the need to make the *catechetical paradigm* more robust. The conceptual distinction of the twentieth century between the *catechetical* and *educational paradigms* of Religious Education is, at this stage, a mere shadow across the landscape.

CHAPTER 2
CATECHESIS IN THE MIDDLE AGES

Catechesis in the Middle Ages, the second historical context, covers a time when major and long-lasting developments in Christian educational thought took place. This section begins with the influence of monastic ideals on education and explores the influence of wider thinking on educational and catechetical thought up to the age of Reformation (*c.* 16th century). The period known, perhaps unhelpfully, as the 'Middle Ages' provides a set of signposts to the key themes of the present book. The changing shape of catechesis at the time marks a gradual rise of broader Christian educational structure and is evidence of the Church's continuing dialogue with other ways of thinking. It is in this period that the Christian message begins to make a significant impact on the cultural landscape of western Europe.

Liturgical and Christian Community Life as Catechesis
    Two issues provide a broad cultural context for this section. First, it is hard to separate catechetical practice for children from wider societal attitudes towards children.[1] Nevertheless, as the Church continued to expand, there remains little evidence of catechetical developments specifically for children. Second, by the seventh century, the collapse of the western

---

[1] See O.M. Bakke, *When Children Became People: The Birth of Childhood in Early Christianity*, 2005. Bakke's argument is that children in medieval times were recognised as more than simply 'adults in the making'.

Roman Empire and the demise of its intellectual patrimony had left very low levels of literacy throughout the lands of its former empire. This state of affairs required the Church to organise its catechetical methods in ways which would be effective for the minimally educated majority of its members.

Crucially, the Church was where people increasingly found the key to the meaning and purpose of their lives.[2] Dedicated catechetical processes were part of the ways in which people absorbed the Catholic faith.[3] Although St Paul had said in Acts 17:24 that God does not dwell in sanctuaries made by human hands, places of Christian public worship grew from the initial Christian homes and Roman *tituli* into a network of churches.[4] Some medieval Church buildings were designed to resemble the *heavenly Jerusalem* with their physical structure and design wholly in keeping with the high eschatological ideals represented by liturgical worship.[5] The Romanesque and Gothic churches and cathedrals became instruments of catechesis – the so-called 'stone bibles' – and examples of wider architectural beauty as pathways to the divine.[6] The liturgical rites performed within and beyond these walls underpinned both the religious formation and the daily life of the Christian community although there is a

---

[2] For a fascinating study of how the Church was an intrinsic part of the life of the people of England before the English Reformation see E. Duffy, *The Stripping of the Altars: Traditional Religion in England c. 1400-c. 1580*. (New Haven and London: Yale University Press, 1992).

[3] It is helpful here to distinguish between how the faith is *taught* and how the faith is *learned*. The former connotes explicit methods designed to teach; the latter includes the more formal aspects of teaching but does so alongside the recognition of wider social and cultural influences on the formation of faith. For more on this, see K. Lawson, Learning the Faith in England in the Later Middle Ages: Contributions of the Franciscan Friars. *Religious Education* 107(2), 2012, pp. 139-157.

[4] K. Baus, The Beginnings. In Jedin and Dolan (Eds.), *History of the Church Vol. 1: From the Apostolic Community to Constantine*, 1980, pp. 59-214.

[5] Cf. K. Seasoltz, *A Sense of the Sacred*. (New York/London: Continuum, 2005) and S. Caldecott, *Beauty in the Word Rethinking the Foundations of Education*. (Tacoma: Angelico Press, 2012).

[6] Pope Benedict XVI, *The Cathedral from the Romanesque to the Gothic Architecture: The Theological Background*. Wednesday Audience, 18 November 2009.

need for caution in drawing too sharp a distinction between life within and without the walls of the church at this time. In late medieval Europe, the religious atmosphere was reinforced with the prominent social role played by guilds, confraternities and pilgrimages in the prayer life of the community with increasingly important roles assumed by the new orders of friars. [7]

Within this overarching atmosphere of religious nurture, there were distinct developments in specifically catechetical practices. Although the Synod of Albi in 1254 had decreed that children of seven years and over should be brought to so-called religious instruction, there was little said about the specific needs of children.[8] For the adults, the scripture-based *narratio* as expounded by St Augustine had gradually given way to a catechetical process centred on the homily at Mass, the recitation of the *Creed* and *Our Father* – and listening to subsequent explanations of these texts. There were concomitant moves to classify knowledge in numerical sets, especially in sets of seven: number of sacraments, deadly sins etc.[9] These are signs of a more systematic approach to Catechesis inspired, possibly, by the seven petitions of the *Lord's Prayer* and the seven *Beatitudes*. In other words, catechesis is organised to facilitate memorisation by a largely illiterate people.[10]

The lack of any extant Church treatise on the theory and method of catechesis from this time suggests that the Church did not apply its mind specifically to developing this issue. Following the example of the early Church, the liturgical and community life of the Church in the Middle Ages continued, broadly, to serve as the principal formational framework for both children and

---

[7] D. MacCulloch, *Reformation: Europe's House Divided* 1490-1700. (London: Penguin Books, 2003); Lawson, 2012.

[8] J. Jungmann, Religious Education in Late Medieval Times. In G. Sloyan (Ed.), *Shaping the Christian Message: Essays in Religious Education.* (New York: MacMillan, 1958), pp. 38-62.

[9] Ibid., pg. 13, pg. 39. See also E. Duffy, *The Stripping of the Altars: Traditional Religion in England c. 1400-c. 1580,* 1992, Ch. 2.

[10] G. Sloyan, Religious Education from Early Christianity to Medieval Times. In G. Sloyan (Ed.) *Shaping the Christian Message: Essays in Religious Education,* 1958, pp 3-37.

adults. In this model, children accompanied their parents to religious ceremonies where they absorbed fully the liturgical atmosphere around them. The initial nurturing role of the parents and the wider family was hence assisted by participation in liturgy and an associated Christian community life.[11]

Christian Education as Cultural Renewal

The conversion to Christianity of the northern Frankish tribes and the crowning of Charlemagne (742-814) as Holy Roman Emperor in 800 was a critical moment in the growth of what was to be called 'Christendom.' Charlemagne sought to renew the continent of Europe through a deepening of Christian culture and belief.[12] The reform of education was at the heart of his ambitious *renovatio*.[13]

The legacy of St Augustine's educational 'philosophy' underpinned Charlemagne's commitment to enact substantial educational reform. [14] Charlemagne's religiously motivated cultural project sought to restore the 'civilization of antiquity' by stressing the importance of education as a culturally unifying force. He was intent on creating a new society which would be underpinned by a more educated and literate population.[15] The *renovatio* created the conditions in which the culture of Europe became fully intertwined with Catholic thought. The term 'Christendom' hence became an apt description for a continent in which education was the handmaid of the Church.

The reforming energy for the *renovatio* was located in the Christian monasteries which had evolved over time to become

---

11 Cf. N. Orme, *Medieval Schools from Roman Britain to Renaissance England.* (New York: Yale University Press, 2006) and E. Vitz, Liturgy as Education in the Middle Ages. In R. Begley and J. Koterski, J. (Eds.), *Medieval Education.* (New York: Fordham University Press, 2005).

12 H. Williams, *Emperor of the West: Charlemagne and the Carolingian Empire.* (London: Quercus, 2010).

13 F.P. Graves, *A History of Education Before the Middle Ages.* (Hawaii: University Press of the Pacific, 1925/2004).

14 E. Kevane, *Augustine the Educator: A Study in the Fundamentals of Christian Formation,* 1964.

15 H. Williams, *Emperor of the West: Charlemagne and the Carolingian Empire.* 2010.

the principal places of Christian education in Medieval Europe. These monastic communities were places where Christian life was nurtured by total absorption into the liturgical life and tradition of the Church.[16]

Alongside the celebration of the liturgy, the monastic communities insisted on the reading of Scripture.[17] St Benedict of Nursia (480-547), the founder of western monasticism, had ruled that his monks should spend some time in this spiritual reading (*lectio divina*) every day.[18] In order to provide reading material for the monks, it was essential to gather and copy some of the great texts from across Europe.

The focus on reading necessitated a promotion of literacy among the members of the monastic communities and, by the 9th century, most Benedictine monasteries had a 'school' attached, although the pupils were mainly potential members of the monastery. The curriculum in these schools was, broadly speaking, a 'liberal arts' education where the study of the Latin and Greek classics, alongside the reading of and meditation on Scripture, became the staple diet of the young scholars. Binding it all together was a continuing focus on wisdom as the ultimate goal of education.[19] The continued emphasis on the value of the liberal arts as pathways to the contemplation of the divine allowed the later medieval mind to see the *ordering* of all knowledge as a way of glimpsing the hand of God in all things.

More broadly, these developments were woven through a related concatenation of social and educational initiatives beginning with the rise of the Cathedral schools and the emergence of the European universities in the second millennium

---

[16] M. Dunn, *The Emergence of Monasticism*. (Oxford: Blackwell, 2000).

[17] Learning to read in medieval times was chiefly, but not exclusively, located in ecclesiastical foundations. See Williams, *Emperor of the West: Charlemagne and the Carolingian Empire*. 2010.

[18] St Benedict, *The Rule of St Benedict in English*. (Minnesota: The Liturgical Press, 1982), Ch. 48.

[19] Hugo of St Victor, *Didascalion*. (New York and London: Columbia University Press, 12th century/1961). (Translated by Jerome Taylor.)

of Christianity.[20] The universities played a major role in the upcoming intellectual controversy over Scholasticism which would leave a profound mark on Catholic thought. The Church, which had been the determining source of influence in medieval Europe, soon had to respond to significant intellectual challenges from other ways of thinking.

The Influence of Wider Intellectual Movements on Catechesis
The encounter between Christianity and the Muslim Empire, which had expanded across Europe in late medieval Europe, was another landmark event in Church history. The consequent 'rediscovery' of the Aristotelian corpus, and the ensuing debate on the place of *Aristotelianism* in Christian thought (the so-called Scholastic debate) was a key moment in the emergence of more *educational* aspects of formation. [21]

Scholasticism as such was an educational *method* which sought to show the inter-relatedness of all Christian doctrine and how this body of teaching was in accord with reason. Hence clerical training in the 'schools' was instrumental in reforming religious instruction for converts according to scholastic lines. Although there is some consonance between this debate and the similar debate over the place of Greek thought in early Christianity, the (perceived) medieval conflict between reason and authority took the debate in a new direction as it seemed to sow seeds of division between learning and the Christian foundations of medieval society.

The work of St Thomas Aquinas (1225-1274) epitomised the Christian position vis-à-vis faith and reason. Western (or Latin) Christianity became increasingly underpinned by his

---

[20] J. Bowen, *A History of Western Education Vol. II.* (London: Methuen and Co. Ltd., 1975), Ch. 2.
[21] There is an abundance of valuable material on these epochal developments, some more accessible than others to the non-specialist. See, for example, the following: A. Nichols, *Discovering Aquinas.* (London: Darton, Longman and Todd Ltd. 2002) and R. McInerny and J. O'Callaghan, Entry on St Thomas Aquinas, *Stanford Encyclopedia of Philosophy, 2005.* http://plato.stanford.edu/entries/aquinas/

pioneering synthesis of faith and reason which had a profound influence on educational thought of the time.[22] Aquinas's focus on the God-given place of reason in the broader educational process hence offered a new perspective on the Augustinian vision of education.[23] Moreover, Aquinas accepted the concept of learning by *discovery*, but reinforced this by emphasising the need to learn by formal *instruction*. This was a significant move towards an approach to learning in which the role of the teacher was that of 'instructor' as well as 'facilitator.'[24]

Aquinas was writing in a cultural context in which attitudes towards children veered between models rooted in the so-called 'depravity' of the child and models rooted in the 'innocence' of children and the related uniqueness of the experiences of the child.[25] This cultural interplay casts a fresh light on the claim that Aquinas was the first to provide a theological rationale for a so-called developmental model of childhood.[26] While verification of these claims requires further study, his *Catechetical Instructions* offer glimpses of a twofold approach involving both faith and reason. For example, in discussing the fourth commandment, Aquinas mentioned the duty of parents to form their children religiously 'without delay', as part of their threefold gift to their children of 'birth, nourishment and instruction.'[27] Nourishment refers in the first place to physical care, but it also infers a nurture approach to education which complements the

---

[22] D. Doyle, Integrating Faith and Reason in the Catholic School. In *Catholic Education: A Journal of Inquiry and Practice* 10 (3), 2007, pp. 343-356.
[23] T. Mooney and M. Nowacki, (Eds.) *Understanding Teaching and Learning. Classic Texts on Education by Augustine, Aquinas, Newman and Mill.* (Exeter: Imprint Academic, 2011).
[24] St Thomas Aquinas, *On Truth Vol II Questions X-XX.* (Cambridge: Hackett Publishing Company Inc., 1994). (Translated by James V. McGlynn.), Question 11.
[25] R. Davis, Brilliance of a Fire: Innocence, Experience and the Theory of Childhood. *Journal of Philosophy of Education* 45 (2), 2011, pp. 379-397.
[26] C. Traina, A Person in the Making: Thomas Aquinas on Children and Childhood. In J. Bunge, (Ed.) *The Child in Christian Thought*, 2001, pp 103-133.
[27] St Thomas Aquinas, *The Catechetical Instructions of St Thomas Aquinas.* (Manila: Sinag-Tala, 13th century/1939), (Translated by Joseph B. Collins.)

instruction which he recommended. This synthesis between nurture and instruction in the rearing of children, with a clear awareness of the value of an intellectual diet (for adults) in the liberal arts domain, is a further and significant development of *catechetical* processes. The importance of cultivating reason was now increasingly fused with the catechetical paradigm.[28]

Scholasticism, however, came under critical scrutiny in the late medieval period from the variegated social and cultural movement known as 'humanism'. The use of the term 'humanism' can be problematic owing to contemporary understandings of 'humanism' as a school of thought which denies the relevance or existence of God. Nonetheless, it is this *classical* humanism which links the early Middle Ages with the Renaissance and the Enlightenment.[29]

Humanism promoted a cultural rebirth (*il rinascimento/le rennaissance*) in which Classical texts were studied in the original languages. More importantly, these texts were deemed worthy of study in their own right and not just as adumbrations of the beliefs of Christianity and/or its ethical code. In Northern Europe this attachment to Classical texts was translated into a religious movement which sought to reassess Christian thought in the light of history.[30]

In essence, Christian humanists sought to re-establish the connection between the perceived simple message of the Gospels and the daily life of the believer. In their eyes, the Scholastic focus on philosophical method had fractured this relationship. This could only be healed, it was claimed, by a return to the study of the Gospels (*ad fontes*) in the original language.

---

[28] Aquinas's contemporary, St Bonaventure (1221-1274) also argued for the place of reason in Catholic thinking.
[29] For more on the Catholic contribution to 'enlightened' thinking, see U. Leher, *The Catholic Enlightenment: The Forgotten History of a Global Movement.* (Oxford: Oxford University Press, 2016).
[30] Once again there is a plethora of material seeking to illuminate this historical moment. See E. Rummell, *Erasmus.* (London/New York Continuum Books, 2004) and I. Bejczy, *Erasmus and the Middle Ages.* (Leiden: Brill, 2001).

The influence of Christian Humanism was exemplified by a Dutch religious order/movement, *The Brethren of the Common Life*, whose focus was education in Christian humanist ways of thinking and living. The movement was initiated by Gerard de Groote (1340-1384). It used the classical educational tools of the liberal arts curriculum to study Scripture and find therein the true message of Jesus which, they claimed, had been obscured by many accretions and human traditions.[31] From this movement there emerged the *devotio moderna* school which, recalling some aspects of the early Christian opposition to dialogue with Greek philosophy, argued that intense study of non-spiritual matters was damaging to a Christian's faith life.[32]

Two works illustrate the influence of this thinking on Catholic spirituality. *The Imitation of Christ* by Thomas à Kempis (c.1379-1471) is perhaps the most famous book to emerge from the *devotio moderna* school, although its intended audience was principally those in the monastic life, not young people. The question of catechesis for children was addressed by Jean Gerson (1363-1429) in *On Leading Children to Christ*.[33] This tract is located clearly in the *catechetical paradigm* and is an application of the principles of the *devotio moderna* to children's catechesis. In response to critics who thought that the teaching of children was beneath his dignity as a university professor in Paris, Gerson saw his work with children as being of equal status to the study of deeper theological issues.[34] Yet a closer reading of his argument suggests that Gerson's preferred model of childhood is not too clear. On the one hand, the child is seen as a delicate plant which needs protecting from evil

---

[31] This movement seems to prefigure trends in scholarship in the 19 and 20th century: the search for the 'historical Jesus' as opposed to the 'Christ of faith'.

[32] "Woe to them that inquire of men after many curious things and are little curious of the way to serve me." (T. à Kempis, *My Imitation of Christ*, (Brooklyn: Confraternity of the Precious Blood, 1954), Ch. 43. This is an example of the principles underlying the *devotio moderna*.

[33] This important text is found in: K. Cully (Ed.), *Basic Writings in Christian Education*. (Philadelphia: The Westminster Press, 1960).

[34] B. McGuire, *Jean Gerson and the Last Medieval Reformation*. (Pennsylvania: Pennsylvania University Press, 2005).

influences. This suggests that Gerson is influenced by the childhood model of so-called religious innocence. On the other hand, Gerson is clear that young children need regular confession owing to their being in a sinful state. In this latter statement, it is not clear if he is referring to a specific group of young people or is making a broader theological statement about children as a whole.

What is noteworthy here is the importance placed by Gerson on the *spiritual direction* of children by means of the sacrament of confession and his stress on the need to teach and guide children with love – although this does not exclude direct instruction in doctrine.[35] It is, in short, an example of the need to include children in the wider catechetical processes and to offer concrete spiritual direction to them.

The range of catechetical and educational developments in the medieval period offers a set of signposts for the argument of the present book. While there is little doubt that the catechetical paradigm remains predominant, what emerges is the growing influence of broader educational initiatives rooted in the desire to nurture Christian faith. The end of the medieval period was a crucial time for the Church as the internal clamour for broader and deeper Church reform was growing stronger throughout Europe. There were other significant geo-political and theological contours to this historical era, the treatment of which are beyond the immediate scope of the present book. These were crystallised in the Protestant Reformation and the Catholic Reform movements, both of which radically altered the shape of early modern Christianity. The influence of the latter on catechesis will be examined in the third historical context.

---

[35] G. Sloyan, Religious Education from Early Christianity to Medieval Times. In G. Sloyan (Ed.) *Shaping the Christian Message: Essays in Religious Education*, 1958, pp. 34-36.

CHAPTER 3
THE CATHOLIC REFORM AND CATECHESIS

The Catholic Reform and Catechesis, the third historical context, explores how the Council of Trent (1545-1563) reaffirmed the principles of Catholic thought in the face of opposition from the Reformed Christian communities of Europe. The key reforms set in motion by the Council prepared the ground for the rise of religious orders and congregations dedicated to education. This provided the foundational blocks for modern educational structures and curricula.

In early modern Europe, population pressure, the pandemics, the rise of the cities and the intellectual discovery of the achievements of classical antiquity all formed part of an atmosphere of intellectual and cultural ferment leading to the eventual dissolution of the medieval order. The moves to reform the Church from within, as well as dealing with external challenges, are a further reflection of a powerful narrative of change and continuity.

The Catholic Reform substantially strengthened the inherited *catechetical paradigm* of Religious Education. The Tridentine Church drew heavily on its own resources, especially Scholastic methods, in order to respond in a resilient manner to the doctrinal and educational challenges it faced from the Reformers.

The Council of Trent and Catechesis
    The Council of Trent was the foremost component of the Catholic Reform. Trent sought to reform many of the abuses

which had taken root in the Church in the two centuries since the Black Death (1346-1353).[1] It promoted unity of faith and defined the key points of Catholic doctrine in the face of opposition from the Reformers. The Council's tools were the Vulgate Bible, the Roman (Tridentine) liturgy, the Code of Canon Law and the *Roman Catechism*.

The Council of Trent saw education as the vital force in the Church's ongoing *internal* reform. There were two aspects to this. First, and in response to the Reformers' desire to use education and schooling as a driver for ecclesial and societal reform, the Catholic Church recognised the necessity of fostering the printed word via printing presses and the construction of ecclesiastical libraries: these were visible manifestation of their prized inherited tradition. Second, and in response to the Reformers' successful focus on the preaching of the Word of God, the art of preaching was given renewed emphasis as a method of catechesis.[2] In the Catholic Church, preaching had been traditionally reserved to members of (certain) Religious Orders. But now the onus was placed on parish priests. This timely shift required suitable preparation of priests and those intending to become priests.

To achieve this laudable goal, a form of Higher Education was established for young men preparing for priesthood.[3] The founding of seminaries was a key moment of the Catholic reform and recognised the comparatively poor state of clerical preaching and, indeed, the apparent deficiencies in the broader cultural and intellectual formation of parish priests throughout the Catholic Church. The seminaries brought together academic studies and a life of piety in a single institution: this was an important indicator of the merging of catechetical and educational paradigms of religious formation. As these seminaries were under the direction of the diocesan Bishop, and not part of the network of universities, the link with the

---

[1] J. Byrne, *The Black Death*. (Westport: Greenwood Publishing Group, 2004).
[2] D. MacCulloch, *Reformation: Europe's House Divided* 1490-1700, 2003.
[3] Council of Trent, Session XXIII. See *Canons and Decrees of the Council of Trent* (Illinois: Tan Books, 1941). (Translated by H. Schroeder), p. 175.

pastoral theme of religious nurture was inevitably highlighted.

Alongside the new initiatives in the formation of seminarians, the Council of Trent aimed to develop the knowledge and skills of the existing corps of parish priests. Hence it proposed that on Sundays and on the principal feasts of the liturgical year, the Bishop and parish priests would catechise the congregations in a manner suitable to the capacity of the audience.[4] It is worth noting that the needs of children were specifically recognised in these directives although without precise details of how this could be done.[5] This seems to be in keeping with the medieval emphasis on the inclusion of the child within the broader catechesis undertaken by the wider community.

In broad terms, the liturgical year would serve as a *leit motif* for this demanding enterprise of catechetical preaching. The devotional life of the Church would, ostensibly, provide the material for a more *scholastic* input in preaching and teaching. Such linking of worship and teaching recalled the teaching mission of the first believers as recounted in the new Testament.

What is significant in the Tridentine age is the development of the earlier focus on community and liturgical life towards a more formal and systematic approach. All of this is centred on the priesthood, preaching and, with the support of groups like the *Confraternity of Christian Doctrine*, the use of printed catechisms. Nonetheless, we need to ask if the

---

[4] ...shall at least on Sundays and solemn festivals either personally, or if they are lawfully impeded, through others who are competent, feed the people committed to them with wholesome words in proportion to their own and their people's mental capacity... (Council of Trent, Session V, Ch. II *On preaching.* Translated by H. Schroeder.)

[5] Preaching is a duty of the Bishop or their delegate, the parish priest. It should be done on Sundays, feast days, and on Lent and Advent either daily or three times a week. The Bishops shall also see to it that at least on Sunday and other festival days, the children in every parish be carefully taught the rudiments of the faith and obedience toward God and their parents. (Council of Trent, Session XXIV, Ch. IV *On Preaching*. In *Canons and Decrees of the Council of Trent.* Translated by H. Schroeder.)

Tridentine emphasis on catechisms diminished the importance of the life of Church community as a formative force. The Jesuit scholar and 20th century catechetical reformer, Joseph Jungmann (1889-1975), has argued that the focus on the written word of the texts and catechisms detracted from liturgy and art as instruments of education.[6] Clearly, the Church sought to *counter* the effects of the Reformation by adopting methods which the Reformers themselves were adopting in their mission to rebuild the Church. Regardless of how we address the concern raised by Jungmann, the historical evidence shows that the community dimension, remained at the heart of the catechetical process. It was given renewed vitality by the Council of Trent which encouraged religious instruction in the vernacular tongue and recognised the differing needs of the members of community.[7]

The Roman Catechism and Catechesis

The 16th century saw a major development in catechesis with the publication in 1529 of Martin Luther's *Catechism*. While catechesis had traditionally operated in preparation for Christian initiation, and was marked historically by active participation in liturgical and Church community life, the advent of the printed catechism reconfigured this tradition by formally setting out key doctrines in a question and answer

---

[6] J. Jungmann, *Handing on the Faith*. (London: Burns and Oates, 1965). (Translated by A.N. Fuerst.) See Context Four in Chapter Four, below.

[7] "That the faithful may approach the sacraments with greater reverence and devotion of mind, the holy council commands all bishops that not only when they shall first, in a manner adapted to the mental ability of those who receive them, explain their efficacy and use, but also they shall see to it that the same is done piously and prudently by every parish priest, and in the vernacular tongue, if need be and it can be done conveniently, in accordance with the form which will be prescribed for each of the sacraments but the holy council in a catechism which the bishops shall have faithfully translated into the language of the people and explained to the people by all parish priests." *Session XXIV, Ch. VII (On sacraments)*. In *Canons and Decrees of the Council of Trent. Canons and Decrees of the Council of Trent* (Illinois: Tan Books, 1941). (Translated by H. Schroeder), p.197.

form. The invention of printing allowed the resultant texts to have a wide circulation and the use of catechisms soon became a distinctive and significant feature of catechesis from the middle of the sixteenth century onwards.[8]

The Reformers' defining desire to promote a 'priesthood of all believers' demanded a (reformed) Church population with the literacy skills needed to have access to the Bible in the vernacular. Interestingly, the Tridentine Catholic Church took up Martin Luther's idea that catechesis should be rooted in a written, detailed account of Christian doctrine.

The systematic organisation of knowledge exemplified in the genre of *catechism* recalled the structure of the medieval encyclopaedia. But now this knowledge base was rooted in Christian doctrine with an explicit apologetic, or confessional, focus.

This process (or system) had its origins in earlier forms of instruction in the Byzantine methods of *erotapokriseis* (question-and-answer) and dialogue.[9] The *Roman Catechism*, however, published in 1566, adopted a discursive, not question-and-answer, style and thus facilitated the further development of the catechism as a specific genre of religious and educational literature alongside its original meaning as a process of Christian instruction.

The aim of the *Roman Catechism*, as stated in its Preface, was to offer a conspectus of the Catholic theological tradition in the context of broader spiritual development. Significantly, the *Roman Catechism* offered clear direction on teaching methodology. In keeping with the approach of the Canons and Decrees of the Council of Trent on preaching and teaching, it recommended a differentiation according to age and capacity.[10] This is

---

[8] J. O'Malley, *The First Jesuits*. (USA: Harvard University Press, 1993).
[9] Y. Papadoyannakis, Instruction by Question and Answer: The Case of Late Antique and Byzantine Erotapokriseis. In S. Fitzgerald Johnson, (Ed.), *Greek Literature in Late Antiquity: Dynamism, Didacticism, Classicism.* (Aldershot: Ashgate, 2006).
[10] It refers to the necessity of differentiation: 'age, capacity, manners and condition demand attention, that he who instructs may become all things

another important sign of an increasingly sophisticated understanding of how catechesis should be developed.

This guide to methodology is a reminder that the *Roman Catechism* was not intended for a wide readership. Its primary audience was parish priests: this group of men was charged with improving the quality of their preaching and instruction by ensuring that they were aware of the theological foundations of the Catholic faith. In a sense, this is an early example of ongoing Professional Development: a timely recognition that all teachers (and the parish priests were also teachers/catechists) need to update their own knowledge base. Hence the *Roman Catechism* could be described as one of the first *teacher's manuals* in education, incorporating material for a structured and detailed curriculum to be adapted according to the needs of the audience.

Given the attention to broader methodological principles enunciated by the Council of Trent[11]there arose the opportunity to consider how catechisms designed specifically for children could enhance their religious formation. One example of this catechetical energy was the triple catechism of St Peter Canisius (1521-1597)which was published around 1555/8 (before the *Roman Catechism*) and, significantly, had three parts aimed at young children, adolescents and young adults. The explicit differentiation of content recognised the developmental needs of young people and their place in the life of a teaching Church. This is a significant indicator that the Catholic Church was responding positively to educational reforms in other Christian communities.

The *Roman Catechism*'s systematic exposition of doctrine was a clear strength, albeit with some limitations. First, its linkage of catechesis with theology laid open the danger of reducing the study of theology to a textbook exercise at arm's length from liturgy and worship. Second, it was not clear if a

---

to all men, and be able to gain all to Christ' (*Catechism of the Council of Trent Preface*: Fourth section).
[11] Council of Trent, *Session XXIV, Ch. VII, On Sacraments.* In *Canons and Decrees of the Council of Trent. Canons and Decrees of the Council of Trent*, 1941.

more doctrinally-focused study of Scripture would impinge upon a *prayerful* reading of the sacred texts in a broader programme of studies centred on the *Roman Catechism*. Finally, the text-book approach, along with the move to classroom or 'Sunday School' style instruction driven by the *Confraternity of Christian Doctrine*, suggests that the study of Christianity was in danger of becoming a largely cognitive exercise separate from the pastoral life of the worshipping Church. This final point is what underpinned the critical historical work of Joseph Jungmann in the 20th century.

These important issues notwithstanding, the importance of the *Roman Catechism* in the history of catechesis should not be minimised. It exemplified a clear progression from the medieval community approach. It retained the traditional four catechetical pillars of Creed, Sacraments, Moral Life and Prayer and successfully incorporated these components within a format designed to counter the doctrinal and structural challenges of the Protestant Reformation. A more systematic and scholastic conceptualisation of Catechesis was developed from this base during the following centuries.

Post-Tridentine Catechesis and the School

In the turbulent years of late 16th century Europe, the Catholic Church and the communities emerging from the Protestant Reformation sought to use education as a key force in their ongoing religious and cultural debates. This was a reflection of the power of education more generally.

The interplay between catechesis and education at this time was strengthened considerably owing to the gradual migration of catechesis to Catholic schools. The Catholic Church's catechetical methods at this time developed the inherited traditions and, in the light of the Tridentine reforms, continued the systematisation of Catechesis alongside the development of broader reforms in education and schooling.

In the centuries after the Reformation, there was an explosion of Catholic religious orders and congregations with a charism for education.[12] The work of the Jesuits and the De La Salle Brothers, for example, reflected the Church's conviction that its growing network of schools would be loci of catechesis. Indeed, such Catholic educational enterprises were the vital link between the education offered by the monasteries/cathedral schools of the Middle Ages and the mass education of the nineteenth century. They continued the reforms in education which, although pre-dating the events of the Reformation, were given renewed impetus by the energy arising from the Catholic Reform. It is here that we find the roots of the modern curriculum, the importance given to the printed word in both textbooks and teachers' manuals and the formation of educators.

The post-Tridentine catechetical and educational reforms were driven by the Society of Jesus. [13] The influence of the Jesuits on education in general rests on their claimed integration of faith and learning. [14] The Jesuits saw their mission as one of correcting the post-Reformation doctrinal confusion by the building of an integrated intellectual and pastoral culture in their growing network of schools. The Jesuits reconfigured the doctrinal heritage of Catholicism into a lasting educational apostolate. This focus on doctrinal orthodoxy within an educational context is evidence of one cohesive paradigm of Christian education which is

---

12 Cf. T. O'Donoghue, *Catholic Teaching Brothers: Their Life in the English-Speaking World 1891-1965.* (New York: Palgrave Macmillan, 2012); R. Po-chia Hsia, *The World of Catholic Renewal 1540-1770.* (Cambridge: Cambridge University Press, 2005) and B. Hellinckx, F. Simon, M. Depaepe, *The Forgotten Contribution of the Teaching Sisters.* (Leuven: Leuven University Press, 2009).

13 For more on this, see A. Scaglione, *The Liberal Arts and the Jesuit College System.* (Amsterdam/Philadelphia: John Benjamins Publishing Company, 1986).

14 Although the Jesuits are not a *product* of the Council of Trent, they were caught up in the general wave of reform which permeated the Catholic world at this time. The formation of Jesuit priests, based on the *Spiritual Exercises* of St Ignatius allied to a rsolidtheological education, was without precedent in religious life at the time. They had thus responded to the Tridentine call for better-formed clergy. Within a very short time, they had become the most influential Catholic order in education.

simultaneously catechetical and educational.

The Jesuit blend of theology and intellectualism covered elementary, secondary and tertiary education.[15] In the *Ratio Studiorum*, the Jesuits set out their vision of an educational system centred on four areas: administration, curriculum, method and discipline.[16] The focus in the *Ratio Studiorum* on the links between cognitive learning and the development of good habits suggests that the Jesuit vision of education was a ground-breaking attempt to marry the best of Scholasticism and Christian Humanism. The Jesuit vision was subsequently enlarged in the educational thought of Giambattista Vico (1668-1744) who, in opposition to the predominance of Cartesian logic in education, reasserted more ancient and abiding forms of the philosophical life rooted in the attachment to instinct, custom, tradition, myth, community, piety and faith.[17]

The innovative pedagogy of the Jesuits was centred on a systematic and progressive arrangement of teaching. In particular, they advocated the practice of an introductory overview/mapping of the subject matter of a particular issue before moving on to a more detailed study of individual components and topics. As such, it is reasonable to infer that specific catechetical classes would have adopted this method. If so, there are clear parallels with the early Christian *narratio* in which the events of Salvation History were presented to the catechumens as part of their gradual journey of initiation. By

---

[15] D. Hamilton, *Towards a Theory of Schooling*. (East Sussex: The Falmer Press, 1989).

[16] This complemented the scope of the *Roman Catechism*: while the *Roman Catechism* set out the religious curriculum as a teaching handbook for priests, the *Ratio studiorum* offered a broader vision of education which encompassed the wider field of studies and amalgamated a number of earlier documents on education by Jesuits thinkers. In fact, the *Ratio studiorum* was nothing less than a handbook for a complete educational system. For a tabulated analysis of the *Ratio*, see J. Padberg, Development of the *Ratio Studiorum*. In V. Duminuco (Ed.) (2000) *The Jesuit Ratio Studiorum: 40th Anniversary Perspectives*. (New York: Fordham University Press, 2000). p. 99

[17] R. Davis, Giambattista Vico and the Wisdom of Teaching. *Asia Pacific Review* 15(1), 2014, pp. 45-33.

the post-Reformation period, doctrine – as presented in the key formulae found in various catechisms – formed a new *narratio* in succession to the Augustinian story-method.

Educational method and the organisation of schools were also key concerns of John Baptiste de La Salle (1651-1719). In common with the Jesuits, De La Salle's vision of education, as set out in his famous work, *The Conduct of Schools,* was an expression of pastoral theology geared towards the spiritual and human needs of the pupils.[18] For example, De La Salle was revolutionary in his vetoing of the use of Latin in favour of the vernacular as the language of instruction. He believed that a knowledge of French would aid his pupils' future *spiritual* growth by enabling them to read a wider selection of Christian doctrine when they had left school.[19] Furthermore, De La Salle favoured a more co-operative and collaborative methodology in the classrooms of his schools. In Catechism classes, for example, the teacher is directed not to speak to the pupils except by way of direct or indirect questions in order to assist their comprehension. De La Salle was keen to avoid a narrow focus on doctrinal tenets bereft of a solid pastoral support system within a Catholic community of learners.

De La Salle's work was a crucial step in the development of a school-based catechesis owing to the emphasis he placed on ordered learning in all subjects. The desire to promote an ordered and pastoral learning environment required a corps of suitably formed teachers.[20] Where the Council of Trent had established seminaries for future priests, De La Salle pioneered the spread of educational centres dedicated to the training of

---

[18] C. Koch, J. Calligan and J. Gros (Eds.), *John Baptiste de la Salle: the Spirituality of Christian Education.* (New Jersey: Paulist Press, 2004). For a classic account of De La Salle's place in the history of pedagogy, see G. Compayré, *The History of Pedagogy.* (London: Bloomsbury, 1905). (Translated by W. H. Payne.)

[19] Ibid.

[20] A case could be made that school teachers and parish priests were the primary agents of the Counter-Reformation in France at this time. See K. Carter, *Creating Catholics: Catechism and Primary Education in Early Modern France.* (Indiana: University of Notre-Dame Press, 2012), 137f.

lay teachers in doctrinal orthodoxy and general pastoral care. This challenged the link between the priest and the catechetical processes which Trent had firmly established, complemented the Tridentine emphasis on the formation of seminarians and, crucially, recognised the importance of the (lay) educator in the broader life of the Church. De La Salle's initiative anticipated the Second Vatican Council's promotion of the universal call to holiness and the later related emphasis on the distinctive vocation of the lay Catholic teacher.[21] This by-passing of the universities as a locus for the 'training' of teachers may suggest that he regarded an overly cognitive approach to the formation of educators as insufficiently pastoral in intent. What is beyond doubt is that De La Salle was offering an innovative perspective on how prospective teachers should be formed.

The Catholic Reform brought together disparate religious practices to form a detailed code of practice centred on the geographical structure of the *single parochial channel* of the diocese with prominent roles afforded to the Parish Priest and Bishop.[22] There is once again no sense of a division between catechesis and Religious Education. The confessionalisation of post-Tridentine catechesis reflected the doctrinal divisions in Christianity but there was little or no questioning of the need for religious faith. This would soon change as new ideas originating in the period now known as the Enlightenment about the validity of the religious experience of humanity would challenge the whole spectrum of Christianity.

---

[21] *Lay Catholics in Schools: Witnesses to Faith*, 1982.
[22] J. Bossy, The Counter-Reformation and the People of Catholic Europe. In B. Luebke (Ed.), *The Counter-Reformation*. (Oxford: Blackwell, 1999).

CHAPTER 4
THE CATECHETICAL RENEWAL
OF THE EARLY TWENTIETH CENTURY

The Catechetical Renewal of the Early Twentieth Century, the
fourth historical context, saw increased demands for reform in
Catholic thinking in catechesis as well as in areas like Scripture
and Liturgy. This multi-pronged movement drew on the
emerging field of educational research and was a crucial
moment in the Church's ongoing reform. It prepared the
ground for the Church's educational reforms which came to
prominence in the final quarter of the twentieth century.

In the years following the Reformation, both Catholic and
Reformed thinkers, although separated in key aspects of
Christian doctrine, were component parts of a society which
recognised the importance of religion. This arrangement was
challenged when the new ideas arising from the Enlightenment
and the French Revolution (1787-1799) questioned the
continuing predominance of the Christian intellectual and
philosophical heritage. [1] Significantly, many Enlightenment
thinkers saw education as the key driver of the people's
liberation from the perceived restraints of revealed religion. [2]

By the late nineteenth and early twentieth century there
was, in consequence, a complex and difficult relationship

---

[1] R. Porter, *The Enlightenment.* (Hampshire: Palgrave, 2001).
[2] A. Podgen, *The Enlightenment and Why It Still Matters.* (Oxford: Oxford
University Press, 2013).

between the Church and the broader cultural climate. [3] Within this fervent intellectual atmosphere, catechesis continued to evolve according to the catechetical and educational paradigms which the Tridentine reforms had inherited from previous centuries. The catechetical and educational paradigms of Religious Education were hence fully part of critical reforms in Church life which took place at this time.

The Catechetical Movement's focus on the reform of catechetical *method* was the fruit of a dialogue with broader thinking in education. This option for reform served as a strengthening of the *educational paradigm* of Religious Education. Furthermore, the Catechetical Movement's focus on the reform of the *content* of catechesis was an attempt to balance the earlier educationally-inspired reforms and foster the catechetical paradigm in the light of advances in liturgical and scriptural scholarship.

The Early Catechetical Movement: The Focus on Method

The determination of the Church to retain catechesis in the school was predicated on an understandable desire to use the classroom as the principal means of halting the perceived de-Christianisation of society set in motion by the Enlightenment and associated ways of thinking. [4] The school, and more precisely the elementary (Primary) school is where the competing forces of Church, society and the modern state struggled for supremacy.

By virtue of the mass schooling arising from urbanization and industrialization, the catechesis of children at the end of the nineteenth century had become, in the main, a school-based activity. It should not be forgotten that the loss of community ritual, itself a doleful consequence of the phenomenon of urbanisation, was a key element in the desire

---

[3] Pope Pius X, *Pascendi Dominici Gregis*, 1907.
[4] It is not the case, however, that the Enlightenment period was universally hostile to religion. There were 'enlightened' Catholics who sought engagement with new thinking. For more on this, see U. Lehner, *The Catholic Enlightenment: The Forgotten History of a Global Movement*, 2016.

of the schools to serve as points of reference for a Catholic population which had been largely displaced from its inherited network of rural religious traditions.

There were certainly many positive aspects to this school-based catechesis, most notably the integral formation which arose from having catechetical classes alongside other subjects in an ordered timetable. More problematic was the continued use of theological categories arising from Scholastic philosophical and theological frameworks with children. When allied to the prevailing use of the Roman and other catechisms as texts to be memorised, this amalgam of methods was a less than effective method for proclaiming the Gospel in a time of intellectual and educational reform.

Against this backdrop, new ideas for reforming catechesis circulated in Europe, especially in Germany. These ideas were influenced in part by the work of the educational theorist, Johann Herbart (1776-1841), who had emphasised the importance of methodology and, in particular, the role of the teacher, in the teaching-learning process. His key point of emphasis was the vital importance of the Lesson Plan in education as this platform was where the teacher, from a position of knowledge, set out how to mould the child, control behaviour and develop learning.[5]

We must bear in mind that the first stage of the catechetical reform was solely a *reform of method* based on the findings of wider educational research. The early catechetical reformers took the existing catechetical practice – based largely on the memorisation of the catechism – and applied Herbartian ideas to it.[6] The results of this reform was a revised catechetical method based on a three-step process of *presentation, explanation*

---

[5] An overview of the Herbartian approach is found in: J. Bowen, *A History of Western Education Vol. III*. (London: Methuen Ltd., 1981).

[6] This involved a lesson-plan based approach which began with Scripture followed by 'text-explanation', usually directed by the catechist/teacher. It ended with the use of the Catechism to explain the point of doctrine set out in the lesson plan.

and *application*.[7] This set the stage for the use of planning sheets to allow the teacher to show in advance how a set of lessons would be developed.

The interplay between catechesis and educational psychology provides important evidence of dialogue between the Church and wider learning in a period when such exchange was often viewed suspiciously.[8] There was some attempt to move away from a purely cognitive approach to learning by engaging with the reality of daily life in the *application* stage of the lesson. However, this method-reform movement did little to challenge the *doctrinal* framework of the catechetical sessions. It continued to emphasise the role of story in catechesis, itself a faint echo of the *narratio* of the early Church. On the whole, the reforms failed to address in any depth issues arising from the intrusion the language of scholastic theology in a process designed to foster the faith of children.

An example of the dialogue with educational psychology is the application of the age of reason debate to the celebration of the ceremony of First Holy Communion.[9] This is seen in the directive *Quam Singulari*, issued under Pope Pius X's authority on 8 August 1910.[10] Pope Pius was keen to dispel the view that Holy Communion was a reward for goodness and virtue instead of the principal *means* to achieve these ends. Hence he allowed young children access to the sacrament of Holy Communion before they had demonstrated a "full and perfect knowledge of Christian doctrine" – while reminding the Church that "the child will be obliged to learn gradually the entire catechism according to his ability". From this evidence, the place of the *Roman Catechism* in Catechesis was not up for

---

[7] The three stage method corresponded to the broader Herbartian approach. For more on this, see B. Marthaler, The Modern Catechetical Movement in Roman Catholicism: Issues and Personalities. *Religious Education* 73 (5) supp. 1, (1978), pp. 77-91.

[8] Pope Pius X, *Pascendi Dominici Gregis*, 1907.

[9] This issue is explored in P. McGrail, *First Communion Ritual, Church and Popular Religious Identity*. (Aldershot: Ashgate, 2007). p. 13 and p. 38.

[10] Sacred Congregation of the Discipline of the Sacraments, *Quam Singulari*, 1910.

debate. Yet there was still a recognised need for differentiation according to aptitude and development. Crucially, the reforms to First Communion enacted by Pius X are another indication of modest reform of the *catechetical* paradigm in the light of dialogue with other thinking. It suggests a more accommodating approach to new ideas than is evident in his robustly anti-Modernist encyclical, *Pascendi,* published in 1907.

In summary, the early stages of the twentieth century catechetical reform evolved in response to dialogue with other disciplines, especially educational psychology. While the radical edge of the early Catechetical Movement was highlighted in its adaptation of Herbartian pedagogy, this radicalism did not yet include a marked sense of the need to reform the content of catechesis. Soon, the second stage of the catechetical renewal would develop a more precise connection between the related Liturgical and Catechetical Movements. This would be concretised principally in the work of the Jesuit priest, Josef Jungmann.

The Early Catechetical Movement: The Focus on Content
By the 1930's there was a change in perspective with regard to the development of catechesis. This second stage of the reform sought to refocus on the perceived joy of the Gospel which had been lost, it was claimed, amidst the learning of layers of theological formulae derived from the *Roman Catechism.* At the heart of this second stage of reform was the strengthening of the links between catechetical renewal and other reform movements in the Church, especially the Liturgical Movement. Religious Education was understood as the continuing proclamation of the Good News of salvation (*Kerygma*) which would, somehow, elicit the response of good living from its subjects.

The key figure of this movement is Josef Jungmann whose work is best understood as an attempt to reclaim the *nurturing heart* of catechesis from the perceived arid scholastic approaches underpinning post-Tridentine methods. At the heart of Jungmann's theology is the intervention of *grace* within the life of the Church. His endeavours to re-imagine catechesis in this light are reflected in two important works in the field: *The Good News Yesterday and Today*, published in 1962, and *Handing on the Faith*, published in 1965.[11] Jungmann recognised the aims and objectives of the early reforms to method but felt that the perceived disproportionate focus on the effective presentation of content skirted round the key challenge then facing the Church's catechetical work: the lack of an appreciation of the concept of Salvation History rooted in knowing, celebrating and living the *Kerygma*, "in all its beauty and in all its supernatural sublimity."[12]

Jungmann objected to the intrusion of largely cognitive approaches to learning in what, he insisted, should be a process of religious proclamation, driven by grace and rooted in the vibrant liturgical life of the Christian community. Such cognitive approaches to catechesis, rooted in part in the Tridentine settlement and contextualised in the polarised religious atmosphere of late sixteenth century Europe and beyond, were, in Jungmann's eyes, an unwelcome imposition of theology and its associated language and methodology on to the catechesis of the young. As a corrective to the perceived dominance of what he saw as the abstract language and intellectual processes of theology in catechesis, Jungmann sought inspiration in a somewhat idealised vision of the early Church which had, he claimed, a "pristine spirit and single-mindedness of its Christian life and in the clarity of its ideals."[13]

Jungmann proposed to strengthen the existing systematic

---

[11] J. Jungmann, *The Good News Yesterday and Today*. (New York: Sadlier Inc., 1962). (Translated by William Huesman); *Handing on the Faith*. (London: Burns and Oates, 1965). (Translated by A.N. Fuerst.) *The Good News Yesterday and Today* was initially published in the late 1930's but did not make a significant impact on the life of the Church until after the Second Vatican Council.

[12] J. Jungmann, *Handing on the Faith*, 1965, p. 36.

[13] J. Jungmann, *The Good News Yesterday and Today*. 1962, p. 17. This approach reflected the late medieval Humanists' desire to return '*ad fontes*' as part of a *renaissance* of interest in early Christianity. Jungmann was in effect adopting the same hermeneutic as the early humanists.

methods of catechesis with a wider vision designed to proclaim the joy (*kerygma*) of the Gospel. For example, he saw the Liturgical Year as a complete course in Christian teaching which presented afresh, through its succession of liturgical feasts, all the key moments of Salvation History. This appreciation of the Gospel message would provide a cultural challenge to Christians whose spiritual life, both personal and corporate, owed more to local customs and a burdensome list of poorly understood obligations.

Jungmann incorporated the vision of the Liturgical Movement in his catechetical work in order to provide an initial synthesis of reform-minded developments. The proclamation of the Christian message could not, therefore, be separated from the liturgy. Such a primary focus on the liturgy enhanced Jungmann's position as a key advocate of a *catechetical* paradigm of Religious Education.[14]

Certain limitations arise from Jungmann's approach, despite its initial appeal. First, the apparent focus on Catechesis as an activity primarily for children sits uneasily with the early Church's focus on adult conversion. More important, however, is the emphasis on the liturgy as means of formation. Although Jungmann never claimed that the liturgy is anything other than an act of worship, it is easy to read into his work a view of liturgy as primarily a pedagogical initiative. In the proposal to learn from and draw on a particular period of Church history, Jungmann was also risking the charge of antiquarianism. While there is a certain degree of truth in his assessment of the 'vivid catechesis' of early Christianity, it is hard to deny the charge of a selective reading of history with little recognition, for example, of the vibrant educational and catechetical developments of late antiquity and the early Middle Ages.

These limitations should not blind the modern reader to Jungmann's contribution to catechesis as a worthy field of

---

[14] See also P.Willey, P. de Cointet and B. Morgan, 2008, for a helpful examination of the connection between liturgical texts and catechetical principles.

study. Recent thinking has developed his original focus on liturgy as the framework for the *Rite of Christian Initiation for Adults* (RCIA). Furthermore, the important place of liturgy in the wider catechetical framework is now recognised in the mainstream of Catholic thought.[15]

By the 1930's, catechetical thought was embarking upon a phase of far-reaching development which would continue throughout the rest of the century. The two-stage reform of method and content reflected the Church's dialogue with other disciplines (method) and its willingness to draw on its own resources in order to address the challenges of the age (content). Catechesis was thus to become a distinct field of study with its own history and an associated need to develop and rediscover its own validatory theoretical corpus. By the middle of the twentieth century there is little sense of Religious Education understood as other than a process of integral faith formation, rooted in a catechetical vision but part of the timetable and framework of the Catholic school. More importantly, there is still no hint of catechesis and Religious Education as separate, although related, conceptual fields, as found in later Magisterial documents.

Concluding Remarks: Part One

Catechetical processes have moved in tandem with wider Church and socio-cultural movements. In the early Church faith formation was centred on the family and the wider Church community in a context of faith nurture. In time this approach was enhanced by greater awareness of the insights offered by Greek philosophy. The work of St Augustine offers a synthesis of the relationship between nurture and scholastic frameworks of catechesis. In the Middle Ages, catechesis retained its roots in the worshipping community and became a component of the *renovatio* of Charlemagne. The rise of the Scholastics ensured that it developed a more cutting *educational*

---

[15] Cf. Pope John Paul II, *Catechesi Tradendae*, 1979 and *General Directory for Catechesis*, 1997: 50, 71, 85, 87, 257, 258.

edge. In the years following the Council of Trent, the Catholic Church organised its catechetical endeavours to strengthen Church identity in the face of the Protestant Reformation. This was the age of the *Roman Catechism* and the rise of the Jesuits and the De La Salle Brothers. Finally, the catechetical renewal of the early twentieth century reformed both the content and the method of catechesis. It set the scene for the insights offered by the Second Vatican Council and the subsequent teaching on catechesis and education from the later years of the 20th century.

This set of historical contexts has demonstrated that the contemporary understanding of catechesis and Religious Education as distinct concepts does not find strong support in the history of Catholic thinking on education. The terms *catechetical* and *educational* paradigms have been used to identify the key moments in this historical journey. The second half of the twentieth century is where the broader articulation of these separate, although related, conceptual fields emerges.

PART TWO
CATECHESIS AND RELIGIOUS EDUCATION
IN THE CONTEMPORARY CHURCH

Up to the early years of the twentieth century there was scant evidence of any firm conceptual dichotomy between catechesis and Religious Education. This arrangement remained in place until the final quarter of the twentieth century when Catholic thinking began, cautiously at first, to consider a new alignment between both concepts. The major shift in Catholic thinking in the years following the Second Vatican Council (1962-1965) had a profound effect on the conceptual framework of Religious Education. During this period, Religious Education developed in response to two currents: the first was the re-discovery of the Christian community (or parish) as the principal site for the diffusion of the Church's catechetical mission; the second was the rise of new thinking in liberal models of Religious Education which contested the concept of faith nurture as an integral component of the school syllabus in an increasingly pluralist society. By the first decade of the 21st century, the historically-conditioned interplay between the *catechetical* and *educational* paradigms of Religious Education had evolved into a fresh understanding of how both concepts were at the heart of the Church's educational mission. This development is charted as follows:

- Developments in Catechesis and Liberal Religious Education (Chapter 5);
- The Magisterium's Response to the New Thinking in Catechesis (Chapter 6);
- Renewing Religious Education (Chapter 7);
- Religious Education: The Response of the Magisterium (Chapter 8).

CHAPTER 5
DEVELOPMENTS IN CATECHESIS AND RELIGIOUS EDUCATION

The method and content reforms of catechesis of the late nineteenth and early twentieth century were followed by a third wave of catechetical reform influenced by the broader educational currents of the age. The new thinking in Religious Education rejected confessional approaches in favour of a more academic study of religion and associated ways of thinking.

The Anthropological Model of Catechesis

The anthropological model of catechesis captured the post-World War II sense of expectation and hope arising from the growth of education and schooling in the industrialised world. There remained, however, a profound ideological debate in the West over the merits of so-called progressive educational thought. These new ideas in education fostered more inductive (student-centred) as opposed to deductive (content-centred) approaches to learning. Within these highly charged political and cultural contexts, new catechetical ideas continued to draw inspiration from the Catholic reform movements of the early twentieth century which had sought to refresh Catholic thinking in the light of the supposed practices of early Christianity.

The anthropological model of catechesis had two key frames of reference. First, it reflected a concern that the Kerygmatic

school's seeming over-emphasis on the proclamation of the
Good News might be interpreted as an anti-intellectualist
stance which favoured a sentimentalism at the expense of
knowledge of a body of received doctrine.[1] Second, it aimed to
tackle the alleged unreceptive attitudes of students, a situation
not wholly unrelated to the social and cultural conditions in
which many lived. This challenge was best addressed, it was
argued, by making contact with people in *all* social conditions
and responding to the pastoral challenges arising from the
levels of material and cultural poverty which impeded any
efforts at genuine evangelisation.

A series of International Catechetical Study Weeks served
as the intellectual and pastoral engine for this new thinking.
These Study Weeks were spread across the years 1959-1968 and
the chosen locations of Nijmegen (1959), Eichstatt (1960),
Bangkok (1962), Katigondo (1964), Manila (1967) and Medellin
(1968) provided an international backdrop.[2] The agenda of the
Study Weeks moved from the initial aim of the adaptation of
the Kerygmatic Movement to the wider objective of the
reform of the Church and its structures. What made this time
particularly interesting is the juxtaposition between the Study
Weeks and the important events of the Second Vatican
Council and beyond. It seemed that the sense of optimism and
hope of the post-World War II world had influenced Catholic
thinkers to freshen Church teaching to meet the signs of the
times and the needs of post-War society.

An example of this move for change was the opening of
the 'Third World' of Africa, Asia and Latin America and the
consideration of how to address the pastoral and social
challenges facing the Church and wider society in those
continents.

Gaudium et Spes provides a primary example of the
acceptance in the Church of the thinking behind the

---

[1] J. Gallagher, *Soil for the Seed.* (Essex: McCrimmon Publishing Co., 2001).
[2] B. Marthaler, The Modern Catechetical Movement in Roman Catholicism:
Issues and Personalities. *Religious Education* 73 (5), supp. 1, 1978, pp. 77-91.

anthropological method of catechesis. Its opening paragraph outlining the "joys and the hopes, the griefs and the anxieties of the men of this age, especially those who are poor or in any way afflicted..." reflects a desire on the part of the Church to align itself with political and cultural shifts in postwar Europe which sought a common home free from the conflicting ideologies which had produced two wars in the space of half a century.

The Study Weeks were influenced by two interrelated but by no means univocal intellectual currents. First, they reflected some of the more radical educational theory of this time which drew on the behavioural sciences as a means of channelling educational outcomes towards the development of the skills and attributes deemed necessary for the continued upholding of the post-war social and economic settlement. Second, they were inspired by the corpus of Catholic social teaching which sought to include improvements in education as part of the mission to improve the living conditions of the poor.[3]

The Study Weeks also offered an ecclesial forum to educationalists like Paulo Freire (1921-1997) who had vigorously challenged the 'banking model' of education for preserving a perceived unjust cultural and economic *status quo*.[4] Freire's thinking was a more radical interpretation of the broader tradition of Catholic social teaching.[5] Within such a wider context, the Study Weeks highlighted the strong political dimension to catechesis at this time. The Medellin Study Week of 1968, for example, located the Church's catechetical work within the Church's broader commitment to social justice; the South American context facilitated an interface between catechesis and the emerging theologies of liberation which

---

[3] Pope Leo XIII, *Rerum Novarum*, 1891.
[4] P. Freire, *Pedagogy of the Oppressed.* (New York: Continuum, 2000). (Translated by Myra Bergman Ramos.)
[5] J. Elias, Whatever Happened to a Catholic Philosophy of Education. *Religious Education* 94 (1), 1999, pp. 92-110. The desire to address economic and social inequalities anticipates some of the impulses behind Pope Benedict XVI's *Letter for the World Day of Peace*, 2012.

were circulating in South America at that time.

Furthermore, the early Study Weeks floated the concept of *Pre-evangelisation* as a way of preparing people to hear the Gospel. This was seen as the first stage of preparing people to hear the Gospel.[6] Fr Alfonso Nebreda (1926-2004), a Jesuit priest and Director of the East Asian Pastoral Institute, clarified further the principle of pre-evangelisation in the context of the new models of catechesis: "The guiding principle of pre-evangelisation is anthropocentric because we must start with the individual as he or she is."[7] This short and important sentence by Nebreda encapsulated the direction in which the catechetical debate was heading. It shows a clear overlap with the Freirian focus on the liberation of the human person from perceived unjust structures.

The anthropological model recognised and gave credence to the different social, cultural and political realities faced by the Church across the world. It drew on the Freirian model of education to propose catechesis as an active agent of ecclesial and social change. In the early 1960's, the Second Vatican Council acted as an official ecclesial forum for the discussion of such views. Many of the ideas emanating from the anthropological model were expressed in its published teachings. In the years following the Council, the growth of the experiential model offered another perspective on catechesis to the Church.

The Experiential Model of Catechesis

The experiential model sought to reorientate catechesis away from the understanding of Divine Revelation principally as the communication of a set of theological propositions towards one predicated on recognition of the life experience and history of the student. In this new model, and in keeping with the student-centred approach of the anthropological

---

[6] L. Erdozain, The Evolution of Catechetics: A Survey of Six International Study Weeks on Catechetics. In M. Warren, (Ed.), *Source Book for Modern Catechetics*. (Minnesota: Saint Mary's Press, 1983), pp. 86-109.
[7] A. Nebreda, East Asian Study Week on Mission Catechetics. In M. Warren (Ed.) *Source Book for Modern Catechetics*, 1983, p. 52.

approach, the student was no longer understood as a *tabula rasa* on whose spirit the words of the Gospel and the *Roman Catechism* would be written. Critics of this form of catechesis claimed (with some justification, it would later emerge) that assorted sociological factors (for example personal history and identity) were perceived as being of higher importance than the receiving of an inherited faith tradition.[8]

The experiential model was a reaction to the alleged dominance of the concept of Salvation History which Jungmann had made the core of his catechetical work. This model had remained at the heart of the Second Vatican Council's document on Divine Revelation – *Dei Verbum*, published in 1965. The experiential construction of catechesis built on the anthropological model and drew on the Second Vatican Council's call for dialogue with other religions to develop a theory of catechesis which had wider implications. Put briefly, if the Church were to accept that some elements of the truth were located beyond its boundaries, did it follow that Truth could not be identified solely with the Church's body of received teachings?[9]

The experiential method also recalled the pedagogical reforms of the early twentieth century (for example, the Munich Method) which had, in turn, drawn on the emerging insights of developmental psychology to improve the dialogue between catechist and student. Furthermore, the experiential model sought to redress the perceived imbalance between the respective emphases of content and method in previous catechetical reforms and allow the student's catechetical

---

[8] Pope Benedict XVI (as Joseph Ratzinger), Handing on the Faith and the Sources of the Faith. In J. Ratzinger, G. Danneels, F. Macharski and D. Ryan, *Handing on the Faith in an Age of Disbelief.* (San Francisco: Ignatius Press, 2006).

[9] Gabriel Moran for example, claimed that Revelation lay at the heart of the student's own faith history. He rejected the traditional understanding of Revelation as a faith tradition to be passed on in teaching and worship. Moran argued that the traditional understanding of Revelation as *sacred history* was no more than a modern construction of the events narrated in Scripture. See G. Moran, *Theology of Revelation.* (London: Burns and Oates, 1967).

experience and personal history to be further enhanced in the light of the new catechetical ideas. In this respect it is questionable if the experiential method was any more revolutionary than earlier methods of catechetical reforms in that it was looking to reconfigure the relationship between so-called cognitive and affective learning with a view to more effective catechesis.

The determined focus on the personal experience of the student encouraged a reconsideration of the importance of teaching doctrine in catechetical programmes. If catechesis had traditionally been focussed on the passing on of a revealed tradition of faith, the more explicit focus on the place of human experience could be interpreted as a new direction within the Catholic tradition.

Taken together, the anthropological and experiential models were wide-ranging attempts to make catechesis more fulfilling and integrated by drawing on a range of insights in the field of education. In practice, both schools of thought recognised the range of human experiences of those to be catechised. Many of the key principles of these models informed the teachings of the Magisterium both in the Second Vatican Council and in the *General Catechetical Directory,* published in 1971.

In summary, the new models of catechesis were designed to improve catechetical practice by drawing both on Church tradition and insights arising from other ways of thinking. This took place as the mode of operation of Religious Education was increasingly questioned by other philosophies and worldviews. This is where it is helpful to explore the genealogy of Religious Education.

Genealogy of Religious Education
'Religious Education' as the title of a subject on the school curriculum has its origin in a particular religious and social context. In the United States of America in 1903, the Religious Education Association (henceforth REA) was founded as a home for Protestant Christians who wished to

reform what they saw as overly pietistic models of religious formation.[10] In this influential movement, Religious Education (also used as the title of the Association's academic journal) was the preferred term for the teaching of Christianity in a way which brought together "liberal theology, the social gospel and progressive education."[11] The emphasis on the *educational* nature of Religious Education was intended to offer an alternative to 'revivalist' tendencies in the Protestant Christian religious instruction of the time. It is here that the roots of a Christian critique of predominantly faith nurture approaches to Religious Education are found.[12]

The intellectual thrust of this movement came from the growing awareness of the child as living organism and not as a figure ready to be pressed into any prearranged form.[13] As such, the REA drew inspiration from the wider progressive movement in American education at that time. Religious Education in its earliest incarnation was not, and never claimed to be, a synonym for religious *instruction*, nor for any explicit Christian nurture approaches to religious formation.[14] On

---

[10] Cf. for example: M. Boys, The Standpoint of Religious Education, *Religious Education* 76 (2), 1981, pp. 128-141 and M. Kravatz, *Partners in Wisdom and Grace: Catechesis and Religious Education in Dialogue.* (Maryland: University Press of America, 2010).

[11] K. Scott, Religious Education and Professional Religious Education: A Conflict of Interest? *Religious Education,* 77 (6), 1982, pp. 587-603.

[12] This fertile ideological movement grew in an America where there was a clear separation between church and state. The separation of powers and the resultant distinction between laws and customs seemed to be a driver of a healthy religious pluralism.

[13] Two important early texts here are: A. Coe, Religious Education as part of General Education, originally published in *The Religious Education Association: Proceedings of the First Convention,* 1903, pp. 40-52 and J. Dewey, Religious Education as Conditioned by Modern Psychology and Pedagogy, originally published in *The Religious Education Association: Proceedings of the First Convention,* 1903, pp. 60-66.

[14] Horace Bushnell's seminal text, *Christian Nurture,* mapped out the key lines of the faith nurture approach within the American Protestant tradition. See H. Bushnell, *Christian Nurture.* (London: T. Nelson and Sons, 1861). For comment on Bushnell, see B. Kathan, Horace Bushnell and the Religious

the contrary, from its outset it sought to offer a new experience located in the encounter between religious ways of thinking and the study of education.[15]

While the REA became more influential in American Protestant circles, the Catholic tradition remained initially unaffected by the issues surrounding the emergence of this new understanding of Religious Education. In the early years of the 20th century, there was no hint that school-based religious instruction was anything other than catechesis and, for good measure, linked to the emerging social teaching of the Church.[16]

Pope Pius X emphasised the teaching of doctrine as a means to personal salvation. His encyclical on catechesis, *Acerbo Nimis*, issued in 1905, offered a template for the systematic teaching of Catholic doctrine. Although written some two years after the founding of the REA in America, Pope Pius X saw clear merit in the didactic approach implied in the English term 'religious instruction'. His own catechism, published in 1908 reflected this way of thinking in its list of simple questions and answers on the key points of Catholic doctrine.[17]

The thematic link between the teaching of Christian doctrine and social reform was picked up by Pope Pius XI. His encyclical on Christian Education, *Divini Illius Magistri*, published in 1929, provided a comprehensive framework for the understanding of Christian Education as an integrated programme of formation with supernatural aims.[18]

The final paragraphs of the Encyclical, however, go in a separate direction to that taken earlier in the century by the

---

Education Movement. *Religious Education* 108 (1), 2013, pp. 41-57 and K. Scott, Religious Education and Professional Religious Education: A Conflict of Interest? 1982.

[15] W. Rainey Harper, The Scope and Purpose of the New Organization. Originally published in: *The Religious Education Association: Proceedings of the First Convention*, 1903, pp. 230-240.

[16] Pope Leo XIII, *Rerum Novarum*, 1891.

[17] *Catechism of Pope Pius X*, 1908. http://www.ewtn.com/library/catechsm/piusxcat.htm

[18] Pope Pius XI, *Divini Illius Magistri*, 1929.

REA. For Pope Pius XI, any educational method which dispensed with the work of grace and relied on human nature is unworthy.[19] Pedagogical approaches arising from too close a partnership with other worldviews presented major challenges to the Catholic tradition.

The lack of a shared understanding of the role of religion vis-a-vis education between the Catholic Church and the REA can be summarised as follows: In the Catholic tradition, the role of 'religious instruction', so called, is to form students doctrinally so that they can enter into dialogue with the world in order to propose a Christian way of thinking. Conversely, the REA's approach is to see Religious Education as a fresh discipline which has arisen from the insights in other fields of learning and, by implication, offers a model for a new way of understanding Christianity. The divergence in understanding as described here provides an insight into the tension between two distinct interpretations of the aims of Religious Education within Christianity.

In time, increasing Catholic membership of the REA played a significant part in its development as a multi-denominational, as opposed to liberal Protestant, organisation.[20] There was, however, no parallel Catholic movement to reconfigure approaches to Religious Education along the lines suggested by the REA. The 'method' reforms of the early catechetical renewal movement valued a more structured and educational approach to catechesis; this reflected, albeit dimly, the educational spirit of the reforms undertaken by the REA.

---

[19] "Hence every form of pedagogic naturalism which in any way excludes or weakens supernatural Christian formation in the teaching of youth, is false. Every method of education founded, wholly or in part, on the denial or forgetfulness of original sin and of grace, and relying on the sole powers of human nature, is unsound. Such, generally speaking, are those modern systems bearing various names which appeal to a pretended self-government and unrestrained freedom on the part of the child, and which diminish or even suppress the teacher's authority and action, attributing to the child an exclusive primacy of initiative, and an activity independent of any higher law, natural or divine, in the work of his education" (Ibid., 60).

[20] J. Elias, Catholics in the REA. *Religious Education* 99 (3), 2004, pp. 225-246.

The Kerygmatic Movement, in its drive to recapture a perceived joy in Christian nurture approaches to religious formation, was a clear move in another direction and a rejection of the philosophy underpinning the REA.

The term 'Religious Education', therefore, is a recent arrival in the Catholic lexicon. Catholic thinking had traditionally emphasised the catechetical and instructional nature of any form of religious formation in the school. It is worth noting that the term 'Religious Instruction' appeared frequently in the English translation of the Magisterial documents on catechesis and education from the first half of the twentieth century onwards. Only later in the twentieth century does 'Religious Education' become the preferred subject title.[21] Indeed both terms are often used interchangeably alongside 'education in the faith' and 'religious training'.[22] What is unarguable is that the use of a broad range of terms to describe the processes of religious formation both within and beyond the school illustrates the complexity of the debate over the most appropriate conceptual framework for Religious Education.

Religious Education as Study of Religion

In the 1960's, the UK based educationalist, Ninian Smart (1927-2001), questioned the value of explicit faith nurture approaches in Religious Education.[23] Also 'on the table', for Smart, were the possibilities offered by cross-border initiatives in religion and education. This seemed to chime with the Church's desire at that time to build bridges with other

---

[21] Cf. *General Catechetical Directory*, 1971, 19; *The Religious Dimension of Education in the Catholic School*, 1988, 66-70 and *Circular Letter to Presidents of Bishops' Conferences on Religious Education in Schools*, 2009.

[22] This varied usage might, of course, reflect the perspectives of the varied authors of these documents over a lengthy period and the role of the translator of Magisterial documents cannot be left to one side.

[23] Smart did initially retain his allegiance to Christianity. For an overview of Smart's religious beliefs, see S. London, *The Future of Religion: An Interview with Ninian Smart*. http://www.scottlondon.com/interviews /smart.html

religious traditions. [24] Smart's body of work reflected a shift from Religious Education as Christian faith formation to Religious Education as a broader study of religious influences on the human condition.[25]

Smart was convinced that Religious Education in schools would be improved by the opening of its conceptual borders, at that time almost exclusively Christian, to the insights into the human condition offered by other religions and their related ways of understanding the world. Smart, whose principal sphere of influence was the English-speaking world, was affected by the patterns of migration which had reshaped the cultural composition of western countries and subsequently driven a concomitant growth in new forms of religious worship.

In his desire to change the face of Religious Education and, in his mind, to strengthen its position in the academic framework of the school, Smart was initially following the reformist lines mapped out by the REA in early twentieth century America. In this way of thinking, a theologically liberal and educationally progressive model of Religious Education was the ideal way ahead. Nonetheless, the REA retained a Christian world-view in its underpinning philosophy. Smart's analysis of the state of Religious Education led, contro-versially, to a diagnosis of 'schizophrenia' arising in part from the juxtaposition between the dominance of nurture-based Religious Education in schools and the provision of Religious Studies in Higher Education (secular) institutions. [26] In response to this situation, Smart's proposed an opening of the language and conceptual framework of Religious Education and theology to wider perspectives and to "the sympathetic

---

[24] The inspiration for this move was *Nostrae Aetate*, 1965.
[25] Cf. G. Moran, Religious Education. In R. Curren (Ed.), *A Companion to the Philosophy of Education*. (Oxford: Blackwell, 2008); The Intersection of Religion and Education. *Religious Education* 69 (5), 1974, pp. 531-541; *Design for Religion*. (London: Search Press, 1974) and *Theology of Revelation*. (London: Burns and Oates, 1967).
[26] N. Smart, *Secular Education and the Logic of Religion*. (London: Faber and Faber, 1968) p. 90.

appreciation of positions and faiths other than its own. Christian theology, in brief, must be open, not closed."[27]

Smart's overall contribution to debates on the nature of Religious Education can be grouped into three strands. First, his recognition of the pluralist nature of society nudged Religious Education away from a confessionalist paradigm which was ill at ease in this pluralist society. Second, Smart was in favour of the neutrality of the state in religious affairs in general: this, too, was an indicator of the desirability of non-confessional Religious Education. Finally, Smart was convinced that Religious Education should evolve into a multi-faith and academically serious study of religions.

Given the broader multi-faceted revolution in Religious Education which took place throughout the 1970's, what was Smart's overall contribution to developments in the field? While there is a shared agreement as to Smart's status as an influential and hugely important figure in the modern history of theories of Religious Education, there is still a debate on how positive his contribution actually was.

Two contemporary scholars of Religious Education, Philip Barnes and Kevin O'Grady, offer contrasting perspectives. Barnes has challenged approaches to Religious Education which are rooted in Smart's ideas.[28] He agrees that Smart's critique of confessionalism in Religious Education is both timely and well-developed. However it does not follow, claims Barnes, that a phenomenological approach is the best, or even an appropriate, response to the challenges posed by confessionalism. Kevin O'Grady, on the other hand, welcomed Smart's ideas on Religious Education. O'Grady sees the Smartian corpus as a pioneering initiative which made contemporary Religious Education more academically respectable.[29]

---

[27] Ibid., p. 91.

[28] Cf. P. Barnes, The Contribution of Professor Ninian Smart to Religious Education. *Religion* 31, 2001, pp. 317-319 and Ninian Smart and the Phenomenological Approach to Religious Education. *Religion* 30, 2000, pp. 315-332.

[29] K. O'Grady, Professor Ninian Smart, Phenomenology and Religious

Other and more profound challenges to Smart's legacy have come from a number of angles. To take one example, phenomenology as parent of cross-religious models of teaching and learning has been deemed inadequate, especially for younger children.[30] An unforeseen legacy of phenomenology, perhaps, has been the removal from the Religious Education curriculum of the conceptual and linguistic resources needed to combat the global threats to the same liberal values which initially inspired Smart's work.[31]

New Thinking in Religious Education in the Catholic Tradition

It is a moot point whether the new ideas circulating in the field of liberal Religious Education influenced the Magisterium. A possible explanation for this might lie in the linguistic barriers separating Rome and the key debates in the field of Religious Education which had taken place principally in English language academic journals.

While it is unlikely that Smart's thinking had any immediate influence on (or were influenced by) the teachings of the Magisterium, his contribution to the intellectual debate on the relationship between religion and education did influence Catholic thinkers like Gabriel Moran. Indeed, Moran's work became a form of conduit for the entry of insights from liberal Religious Education into Catholic intellectual life - although it would be unwise and unjust to Moran himself to interpret his substantial body of writings solely in terms of his interpretation of the 'mind' of Ninian Smart. The importance of Moran's work for any discussion on contemporary Religious Education comes from his Smartian vision of Religious Education as an academic field with outposts well beyond the confines of the Catholic Church and any other named Christian tradition. Moran's understanding of

Education. *British Journal of Religious Education* 27 (3), 2005, pp. 227-237.
[30] J. Hull, *Studies in Religion and Education*. (London: The Falmer Press, 1984).
[31] J. Conroy and R. Davis, Citizenship, Education and the Claims of Religious Literacy. In M. Peters, A. Britton and H. Blee (Eds.), *Global Citizenship: Philosophy, Theory and Pedagogy*. (Rotterdam: Sense Publishers, 2007).

the nature of Religious Education needs prefacing, however, by further terminological precision. To be clear, Moran preferred the term 'crisis *of* Religious Education' to 'crisis *in* Religious Education'.[32] The former term was, he believed, a more meaningful articulation of the need to redefine Religious Education based on the insights offered by education and rationality. The latter term, in contrast, suggested a return to debates on the alleged doctrinal weaknesses of Religious Education in the post Second Vatican Council Church.

Moran drew on this terminological distinction to propose a new conceptual model of Religious Education. He favoured 'ecumenical education' (the words are part of the title of his book) as the descriptor of a new conceptual framework for a subject which would be developed by co-operation between those who were searching for a truth that was greater than any single truth professed by individual religions. Moran's understanding of 'ecumenical' in this case is interesting. He seems to be proposing a model of Religious Education rooted in a framework transcending any firm attachment to a named religious tradition. For Moran, the benefits of this model included a move away from the *preacher model* (i.e. faith nurture) of Religious Education and a willingness to engage with topics other than Scripture and Dogma.

In time Moran took a far more challenging stance against Church-centred Religious Education. In particular, he labelled traditional Religious Education as "ecclesiastical thought-control for children" and saw the new discipline of 'Religious Education' as a way to encourage much-needed changes in the structures of organised religion.[33]

Magisterial teaching shows little sign of Moran's influence. Sr Finola Cunnane, however, drew on Moran's thought in an attempt to understand better the nature and purpose of Religious Education for the modern world. Cunnane shares

---

32 G. Moran, *Design for Religion.* 1971, p.12.
33 G. Moran, The Intersection of Religion and Education. *Religious Education* 69 (5), pp. 532-533.

with Moran the view that Religious Education cannot be a component part of the catechetical process if it is to remain true to its identity as an academic subject.[34] She rejects outright the possibility of accommodation between faith nurture and educational structures. Cunnane's perspective on the academic underpinning of Religious Education reflects, albeit very dimly, Pope Paul VI's call in *Evangelii Nuntiandi* for "systematic religious instruction".[35] Cunnane proposes an academic process, which implies some form of systematic approach, but with a wholly divergent conceptual understanding of Religious Education and its associated objectives for learning. The focus in contemporary Magisterial teaching on Religious Education is to give pupils "knowledge about Christianity's identity and Christian life".[36] This is a firm response to those seem to have advocated otherwise.

Cunnane's work summarises Moran's thinking in a twenty-first century context. For Smart, Moran and Cunnane, Religious Education is best understood as a developing subject which flourishes when liberated from the (perceived) limitations of faith nurture conceptual frameworks. Alongside this limited model, further radical thinking emerged in the 1970's and 1980's. This school of thought sought a suitable template for an educational paradigm of Religious Education which was distinct from wholly catechetical and faith nurture frameworks yet recognised the contribution that effective Religious Education played in the student's own faith journey.

---

[34] "Teaching religion in schools is an important aspect of schooling in Religious Education. Teaching religion in a classroom is an academic process. It is not concerned with initiating people in religious matters. Neither is it preoccupied with teaching a person a religious way of behaving" (F. Cunnane, *New Directions in Religious Education*. Dublin: Veritas, 2004), p. 136).

[35] Pope Paul VI, *Evangelii Nuntiandi*, 1975, 44.

[36] *Circular Letter to Presidents of Bishops' Conferences on Religious Education in Schools*, 2009, 17.

CHAPTER 6
THE MAGISTERIUM'S RESPONSE TO THE
NEW THINKING IN CATECHESIS

The catechetical reform movement was given further impetus by the Second Vatican Council's seeming embrace of the claims made by the Church reform movements of the early years of the 20th century. The tone of the *General Catechetical Directory*, published in 1971, chimed with the progressive educational thought of the time. In due course, further reforms in catechesis counteracted a perceived deficiency in doctrinal knowledge while retaining some insights from the anthropological and experiential models of Catechesis.

The Growth of Inductive Catechesis: The Second Vatican Council and Catechesis

By the time of the Second Vatican Council, *pace* the insights arising from the catechetical reform movement, the *catechetical underpinning* of Religious Education, as outlined by Pope Pius XI's *Divini Illius Magistri*, remained the principal conceptual framework.[1] Interestingly, the Council did not produce a document dedicated to catechesis. This omission, if we can call it that, seems curious given the intellectual energy surrounding the International Study Weeks taking place around the time of the Council. Perhaps the Church was not

---

[1] Pope Pius XI, *Divini Illius Magistri*, 1929. To date, this is the only encyclical on education.

yet in a position to re-evaluate the traditional doctrinal focus of Catechesis and was exercising an understandable caution in the face of the new thinking around catechetical matters. Nevertheless, two contrasting points about Catechesis emerge from reflection on the wider teachings of the Council.

First, the Council reminded all Bishops that Catechesis was their responsibility as chief pastors of the local Church. Bishops were called to develop catechetical programmes based on the foundations of "holy scripture, tradition, liturgy and on the teaching authority and life of the Church." [2] The focus on the role of the Bishop articulates an understandable desire to keep the supervision of catechetical thought within the borders of the faith tradition and, perhaps, limit the influence of other and seemingly more radical voices in the wider debates about aims and purposes of education.[3]

Second, the wider theme in the Second Vatican Council of openness to other ways of thinking encouraged a reassessment of how best to deal with growing societal change. The claim of openness to the wider world and its associated ways of thinking needs reading in a broader theological and educational context. In essence, the nature of Revelation was at the heart of the discussion. The Council's Dogmatic Constitution on Divine Revelation, *Dei Verbum*, had reiterated the traditional understanding of Revelation as a set of doctrinal propositions centred on the Paschal Mystery.[4] This left the Church open to charges of a perceived slant towards an overly cognitive approach to teaching. It is no easy task to reconcile the insights of *Gaudium et Spes* with the more traditional view of Revelation found in *Dei Verbum*. On the one hand, *Dei Verbum* taught that Truth was found in the revealed doctrine of the Catholic Church yet in *Gaudium et Spes*

---

[2] Second Vatican Council, *Christus Dominus,* 1965, 14.

[3] More recently, Pope Francis has reminded the Church that the life of the believer is "a life lived in the Church"; this ensures that catechesis and theological study are partners in the Church's mission to transmit its heritage to new generations. See Pope Francis, *Lumen Fidei,* 2013, 22.

[4] Second Vatican Council, *Dei Verbum,* 1965, 3-8.

there is an openness and a willingness to learn from various situations arising in the world. This juxtaposition is further encapsulated in *Lumen Gentium*'s claim there is only one Church of Christ subsisting in the Catholic Church while "other elements of sanctification and of truth are found outside its visible confines." [5]

Given these contrasting views and the debates they engendered, it is not surprising that the years following the Council saw continued radical thinking in Catechesis. There were now moves to engage with insights from beyond the Catholic and the broader Christian tradition, as found in the experiential model of Catechesis

Responding to the Catechetical Movement: The General Catechetical Directory

The publication in 1971 of the *General Catechetical Directory* (henceforth GCD*)* was a landmark occasion. The catechetical reforms which had begun on the fringes of the Church were gradually – and not without debate –assimilated into Church teaching and practice over the twentieth century. This reforming energy had now coalesced into the core of a document which would, in principle, guide all catechetical endeavours for the following twenty six years. The GCD highlighted the scale of the cultural challenges facing the Catholic Church in the late 1960's and early 1970's and, in response, offered some contrasting lines of thought with Pope Pius X's *Acerbo Nimis,* issued in 1905.

The Second Vatican Council had not mandated a new catechism. It did, however, decree that "general directories" concerning the care of souls be compiled. [6] The innovative genre of a *directory* was a way of sharing authority with local Bishops in fields such as catechesis, in line with the principles of *communio.*

The Council was also taking into account broader

---

[5] Second Vatican Council, *Lumen Gentium*, 1964, 8. It is not possible to do justice to this debate in a short volume on education.
[6] Second Vatican Council *Christus Dominus*, 1965, 44.

educational trends to move away from an over-reliance on codified and centralised curricula towards seemingly more democratic, or decentralised, approaches.

The new genre of directory was not co-terminus with catechism. It suggested a text with a looser structure, yet still identified with the authority of the universal Church. These directories would include one with a special responsibility for "catechetical instruction of the Christian people" and deal with all matters pertaining to this enterprise, including the preparation of suitable books.[7] Interestingly, this choice of words does not rule out a new catechism.

The publication of the GCD marked a radical shift away from the traditional use of catechisms in teaching. Following the insights of so-called progressive elements in education, the GCD favoured the *inductive* method (from below) over the *deductive* method (from above) of catechesis. It claimed, for example, that the *inductive* method was an accurate reflection of the original preaching methodology of Christ.[8] While this observation reflected the acceptance of the insights of the wider catechetical and educational currents, it did leave the GCD open to accusations of partiality since the teaching methods of Jesus as recorded by Scripture cannot be fully identified with any one 'school' of educational thought.

The GCD emphasised the nexus between evangelisation and catechesis in the broader context of the pastoral ministry of the Word. It reasserted the role of the wider parish community in catechesis. Although it acknowledged the traditional role of the school in religious formation, it had little to say about the nature of Religious Education apart from the brief observation that in the older Christian countries (meaning Europe) "Catechesis often takes the form of religious instruction imparted to children or adolescents in school or outside of school."[9]

7 Ibid.
8 *General Catechetical Directory*, 1971, 72-74.
9 *General Catechetical Directory*, 1971, 19.

This line of thinking can be interpreted in three ways: a) there was no urgent need to reform Religious Education; b) as a document dedicated to catechesis, the GCD did not see a *school* subject as falling within its terms of reference and c) catechesis and Religious Education (or instruction) were synonymous concepts with the only difference being one of location. There is an element of truth in each of these observations.

Pope Pius X had recalled the Council of Trent's framework for Catechesis in which Parish Priests had been encouraged to develop wide-ranging catechetical programmes to counter the widespread religious ignorance of the time.[10] The GCD, however, moved in a different direction. It saw the need to move beyond an improved *in-house* catechesis in order to address the wider cultural challenges facing the Church. The shift in emphasis would seem to be a recognition that the catechetical renewal called for by Pope Pius X had failed. The GCD affirmed the position of those who had advocated new models of catechesis as a way of countering the perceived deficit in Christian formation arising from older models formation.

The GCD also marked the move from *Catholic uniformity* to *inculturation* arising from the influence of the anthropological and experientialist models of catechesis, as advocated in the 1960's. The renewal of catechesis became a priority for the Church and responsibility for the implementation of the new thinking was given to local Bishops' Conferences.[11]

---

[10] Pope Pius X, *Acerbo Nimis*, 1905, 11-12.

[11] The new role of Bishops' Conferences had originated in the Second Vatican Council's reorientation of the decision-making processes of the Church. Its support for the formation of a Synod of Bishops was a recognition of a perceived need to appear more open to the emerging Church in the developing world and to be less centralist in its decision-making processes. A good example of the contribution of a Bishop's Conference to the catechetical debate was the Italian Bishops' Conference's publication of *Il Rinnovamento della catechesi* (CEI 1970). This document was translated into English with the title *Teaching the Faith The*

The growth of this more inductive method of catechesis did not go unopposed. By the middle of the 1970's the Magisterium had begun, cautiously at first, to re-assess the shape of catechesis and the importance of teaching doctrine.

The Recovery of Religious Instruction

By the late 1970's the Magisterium sought to recover a more deductive model of catechesis in order to counteract perceived deficiencies inherent in the new catechetical methods which had emerged in the years following the Council. At the heart of this was a concern over the seeming downgrading of traditional doctrinal instruction.

The recovery, so to speak, of a more didactic (or deductive) approach to catechesis had four related stages:

(i) Pope Paul VI made a clear link between catechesis, evangelisation and religious instruction in his 1975 Apostolic Exhortation, *Evangelii Nuntiandi*;

(ii) Pope John Paul II cautioned against forms of catechesis which, in both content and method, were not aligned with the teaching of the Magisterium;

(iii) the genre of the catechism returned, so to speak, with the publication of the *Catechism of the Catholic Church* in 1992 and the *Compendium of the Catechism of the Catholic Church* in 2005;

iv) the publication of the *General Directory for Catechesis* (GDC) in 1997 harmonised the various strands of catechetical thought. All four elements will be explored below.

i)   Catechesis and Evangelisation

The important role of the Bishops in the development of strategies for evangelisation and catechesis was further highlighted by Pope Paul VI's convocation of two important Synods of Bishops.

New Way (Catholic Bishops' Conference of England and Wales 1973). The *Introduction* reflected a desire to maintain an integrated vision of education. There was, as yet, little hint of future developments in the conceptual framework of Religious Education in the Catholic school and its relationship with Catechesis.

The first of these Synods met to discuss evangelisation and led to Pope Paul VI's *Evangelii Nuntiandi*. In this document, the Pope issued a heartfelt call to locate the Church's catechetical mission within the broader picture of evangelisation. Interestingly, he defined catechetical instruction as a means of evangelisation to serve the whole Church.[12] In this important text, Pope Paul VI reminded the Church that the body of teaching which it had received should be preserved and taught afresh to new generations using the best pedagogy on offer.

The call for "systematic religious instruction" was a warning against forms of catechesis which veered too close to experientialism. For Pope Paul VI, catechesis found its roots in the traditions of the past but remained in need of constant development. Given the suspicion, and at times hostility, in educational circles of the 1960's and 1970's to traditional forms of teaching and learning, the advocacy of "systematic religious instruction", with its suggestion of a course of studies taught didactically, was (and remains) a profoundly counter-cultural statement.

This methodological preference recalled the deductive approach and tone of the *Roman Catechism*. It recognised the many layers of tradition in the Church's own history while retaining the notion of episcopal authority in the approval of suitable texts. In recalling the Church's commitment to the teaching of its own doctrinal heritage, Pope Paul VI also put down a marker against those who wished education more

---

[12] "A means of evangelisation that must not be neglected is that of catechetical instruction. The intelligence, especially that of children and young people, needs to learn through systematic religious instruction the fundamental teachings, the living content of the truth which God has wished to convey to us and which the Church has sought to express in an ever richer fashion during the course of her long history No one will deny that this instruction must be given to form patterns of Christian living and not to remain only notional. Truly the effort for evangelisation will profit greatly – at the level of catechetical instruction given at church, in the schools, where this is possible, and in every case in Christian homes – if those giving catechetical instruction have suitable texts, updated with wisdom and competence, under the authority of the bishops" (Pope Paul VI, *Evangelii Nuntiandi*, 1975, 44).

broadly to be less 'traditional' and 'progressive'.[13] Without doubt, this was a radical position to take at the time.

More broadly, *Evangelii Nuntiandi* followed the GCD of 1971 in blending what were the traditionally separate but related concepts of evangelisation and catechesis into one process of Christian formation. This conceptual revision acknowledged the place of the school in religious formation, while situating catechesis primarily in the wider processes of evangelisation. Given that the traditional framework of Christian initiation had seen catechesis as subsequent to evangelisation, the reconfigured approach was a reflection of new thinking in the field. Significantly, the role of the school is not explored in any depth. There is no indication of the future developments which would lead to a reappraisal of the relationship between catechesis and Religious Education in the school.

ii)   Catechesis as an Ecclesial Mission

The Second Synod of Bishops in 1977 had Catechesis as its theme and led to the publication in 1979 of Pope John Paul II's Apostolic Exhortation *Catechesi Tradendae*. Pope John Paul II followed Pope Paul VI in recognising the challenges arising from weak forms of catechesis. He regarded effective catechesis as an indispensable feature in the Church's ongoing implementation of the work of the Second Vatican Council.

Regarding catechesis and the Catholic school, Pope John Paul II affirmed that "the school provides catechesis with possibilities that are not to be neglected."[14] This line of thinking is clearly informed by *Evangelii Nuntiandi*'s comments on the nexus between catechesis and the school.[15] It mirrors the GCD's portrayal of catechesis within the school setting and reminds the Church that the Catholic school should offer high-quality religious instruction as part of its curricular provision.

---

[13] See J. Bowen, *A History of Western Education Vol. III*, 1981, pp. 543-550.
[14] Pope John Paul II, *Catechesi Tradendae*, 1979, 69.
[15] Pope Paul VI, *Evangelii Nuntiandi*, 1975, 44.

In order to develop catechetical processes, Pope John Paul II proposed a balanced methodology which eschewed routine and embraced genuine renewal from within the ecclesial tradition. In practical terms, he called explicitly for a rediscovery of "the human faculty of memory" as a way of integrating "the great events of the history of salvation" in the collective consciousness of the Church, thus recalling the early Church's focus on the *narratio* as a pedagogical method.[16] In so doing, he reiterated Pope Paul VI's call in *Evangelii Nuntiandi* for a "systematic religious instruction" to preserve the memory of the Christian tradition at the heart of the Church. Pope John Paul, however, goes a stage further in advocating memorisation as a tool of Catechesis alongside dialogue, silence and written work.[17] Again let us not underestimate how radical a proposal this was at the time.

Pope John Paul II identified both the successes and the limitations of the new thinking in catechesis. He recognised the challenges arising from an eclectic approach driven in part by individual catechists' selection of what was, and was not, important. Given the wider educational climate of the time, it is no surprise that many in the Church viewed with suspicion moves to regulate such matters in line with a perceived traditionalist approach to teaching. [18] Pope John Paul II, however, recognised that a loose approach to catechesis was not in keeping with authentic catechetical tradition. Indeed, he hints at the necessity and indeed the desirability of some form of normative text to limit more speculative approaches to catechesis and theological study.[19]

---

[16] Pope John Paul II, *Catechesi Tradendae*, 1979, 55.

[17] This blend of methods accords with the broader notion of education as the exploration of the treasures of human knowledge in contrast to methods overly driven by predetermined outcomes.

[18] This highly contentious topic is covered in M. Wrenn, *Catechisms and Controversies: Religious Education in the post-Conciliar Years.* (San Francisco: Ignatius Press, 1991) and M. Wrenn and K. Whitehead, *Flawed Expectations: The Reception of the Catechism of the Catholic Church.* (San Francisco: Ignatius Press, 1997).

[19] "Thus, no true catechist can lawfully, on his own initiative, make a selection of what he considers important in the deposit of faith as opposed

iii) *The Catechism of the Catholic Church:* A Normative Text for Catechesis

As noted above, the anthropological and experientialist models of catechesis had not been universally welcomed in the Church. There was a perception that the post-Vatican II catechetical focus had been weighted too heavily in favour of a *horizontal* (or overly-inductive) dimension which, in its more extreme manifestations, regarded the systematic teaching of revealed Christian doctrine as an unwelcome leftover from the so-called pre-Vatican II Church. The then Cardinal Joseph Ratzinger shared the views of those who sought a reshaping of the catechetical landscape in order to counter widespread religious illiteracy.[20] In particular, he expressed profound regret at the removal of the genre of the catechism from religious teaching and the related questioning of the relationship between method and content in catechesis.

In response to the general concerns raised about the general level of doctrinal awareness, the Synod of Bishops of 1985 recommended the publication of a new catechism to serve as a point of reference for all future catechisms, or compendia, of doctrine throughout the Church.[21] This recommendation reflected Pope John Paul II's call in *Catechesi Tradendae* for the introduction of some form of normative doctrinal text to serve as point of reference for catechists.

The *Catechism of the Catholic Church* (henceforth CCC) was eventually published in 1992. As the *Roman Catechism* was written in the context of, and indeed called for by, the Council of Trent in the 16th century, the CCC was written in the

---

to what he considers unimportant, so as to teach the one and reject the other" (Pope John Paul II, *Catechesi Tradendae*, 1979, 30).

[20] Pope Benedict XVI, (as Joseph Ratzinger), Handing on the Faith and the Sources of the Faith. In J. Ratzinger, G. Danneels, F. Macharski and D. Ryan, *Handing on the Faith in an Age of Disbelief*, 2006), p. 16.

[21] "Very many have expressed the desire that a catechism or compendium of all Catholic doctrine regarding both faith and morals be composed, that it might be, as it were, a point of reference for the catechisms or compendiums that are prepared in the various regions" (Second Extraordinary Synod of Bishops, 1985, II, B, A4). https://www.ewtn.com /library/ curia/ synfinal.htm.

context of the reforms mandated by the Second Vatican Council and the GCD's call for the preparation of new catechetical texts.[22]

The primary audience of the CCC is the Bishops of the Church and, by extension, all priests and those with an interest in catechesis. This is similar to the claim of the *Roman Catechism* to serve as a manual for parish priests but the CCC has a wider scope: all catechists are its target audience. In the claim to serve as a reference point for catechisms composed in other countries, there is a recognition of the universal-local dimensions of the Church.

Although the CCC allowed greater freedom to local Churches to compose their own catechisms, the CCC's historical significance lies in its counter-cultural exposition of a body of revealed doctrine to be placed at the heart of the catechetical life of the Church.[23] It is hence an official response to Pope Paul VI's call for the recovery of strong forms of religious instruction. It seemed that the catechetical landscape had shifted towards an embrace of more deductive models.

The Magisterium heeded its own advice to use the CCC as a primary source for other catechetical texts. The publication of the *Compendium of the Catechism of the Catholic Church* in 2005 illustrated the ongoing development of catechetical thinking.

There are three points worth noting here. First, as a derivative text, the *Compendium* followed the order and structure of the CCC but reconfigured the doctrinal sections to create a question-answer style text designed to facilitate memorisation of short focussed doctrinal statements. While this reflected Pope John Paul II's call for "memorisation", it also raised the legitimate question of whether a more cognitive approach to religious instruction was a denial of the perceived

---

[22] *General Catechetical Directory*, 1971, Introduction.
[23] There is no sense that the *Catechism of the Catholic Church* was intended to be a centralised doctrinal straightjacket; on the contrary, it is written as a reference book for catechists and not as a template for all forms of Catechesis.

benefits arising from the anthropological and experiential models of catechesis.

Second, the *Compendium* was explicit in its use of religious art as a pedagogical tool. This was a reminder of former times when art illustrated the stories of Scripture for the mainly illiterate Church congregations. In its inclusion of this traditional catechetical methodology, the *Compendium* broadened its appeal and complemented the use of the memory and the associated cognitive dimension to Catechesis.

Finally, the *Compendium* included a section of prayers. This placed the apparent cognitive dimension of learning in the wider context of Christian prayer, recognising that the ultimate purpose of learning is, for the Christian, a right relationship with God arising from a balance between the cognitive and affective dimensions of learning.

Before the publication of the *Compendium*, the Church had already addressed the need to support the doctrinal pillars of the CCC with a revised set of pastoral directives for Catechesis. This was in recognition of the changes in the Church and society since the publication of the GCD. The new directory was a timely and comprehensive map of the challenges and opportunities which the Church needed to address in order to support all involved in the vital task of religious formation

iv)   *The General Directory for Catechesis*: Exploring Catechetical Methods

If the GCD was a partner volume to the teachings of the Second Vatican Council, the *General Directory for Catechesis* (GDC) of 1997 was a companion volume to the *Catechism*. It was a necessary updating of the earlier GCD in the light of developments in educational and catechetical thought.

Following its parent publication of 1971, the CDC recognises the limits of the genre of a catechetical directory. It can offer no more than broad lines of pastoral guidance.[24] In this vein, it directs its vision to the Bishops of the Church and

---

[24] *General Directory for Catechesis*, 1997, 9.

all involved in catechetical initiatives with the expressed hope that it would serve as a reference point for future catechetical texts, including the publication of local directories and catechisms.[25]

The GDC affirms the delicate balance between catechesis as both a necessary element of evangelisation and a transmission of a body of doctrine.[26] While criticisms of a 'light touch' doctrinal focus in the 1970's and 1980's had some validity, the wider pastoral approaches arising from the anthropological and experientialist approaches to catechesis were not to be too easily discarded.

It is important to note that there is little indication in the GDC that catechesis was synonymous with, or even related to, Religious Education. The few paragraphs afforded to the role of the Catholic school in catechesis reflect the primacy of the wider Church community (*parish*) and not the school, as the centre of the catechetical enterprise.

The role of the Catholic school is dealt with in two paragraphs (259-260) in the final section of the document under the heading 'Catechesis in the Particular Church'. This section recognises the important role of the Catholic school in the life of the Church and draws on *Catechesi Tradendae* where the vital role of religious instruction in the Catholic school had been emphasised.[27] There is little sense here of a school-based

---

[25] Ibid., 11.

[26] "The publication of the Catechism together with the aforementioned interventions of the Magisterium necessitated a revision of the *General Catechetical Directory* so as to adapt this valuable theologico-pastoral instrument to new situations and needs. It is in service of the entire Church that the Holy See now seeks to collate this heritage and to organize it systematically in order to make it available for catechetical purposes" (*General Directory for Catechesis*, 1997, 7).

[27] "Religious instruction in schools is developed in diverse scholastic contexts, while always maintaining its proper character, to acquire different emphases. These depend on legal and organisational circumstances, educational theories, personal outlook of individual teachers and schools as well as the relationship between religious instruction in the schools and family or parish Catechesis" (*General Directory for Catechesis*, 1997, 74.)

catechesis model and the recognition given to both catechesis and religious instruction offers a wider ecclesial context for their respective modes of operation.[28]

It needs, of course, to be borne in mind that the GDC was written after the Magisterial documents on education had proposed that catechesis and Religious Education be considered as separate although related enterprises. The explicit recognition of the distinction shows a common approach between the Congregation for the Clergy ('author' of the catechetical directory) and the Congregation for Catholic Education (author of the documents on education). The dual approval, so to speak, lends considerable weight to the established Magisterial *distinction* between catechesis and Religious Education.

The renewed focus on the parish as the key locus of faith formation raised further questions about the role of school regarding the religious nurture of young people. This led to a rethinking of the conceptual framework of Religious Education and its relationship with catechesis and the wider Church.

---

[28] "Christian education in the family, Catechesis and religious instruction in schools are, each in its own way, closely interrelated with the service of Christian education of children, adolescents, and young people" (Ibid., 76).

CHAPTER 7
RENEWING RELIGIOUS EDUCATION

In the time between the Second Vatican Council (1962-1965) and the publication of the *General Catechetical Directory* in 1971, the new thinking in catechesis did not deal directly with the question of Religious Education. Soon, such fresh thinking began to effect some modest reform in how to develop Religious Education. This is the seed of a renewed understanding of the subject.

Catechesis and Religious Education: An Uneasy Relationship
The nature of the relationship between catechesis and Religious Education came under critical scrutiny in the years following the publication of the GCD in 1971. This took place against a twofold backdrop: a) the traditional faith-nurture approach to a school subject seemed increasingly out of place in a pluralist society and b) internal Church reform had shifted the catechetical focus away from the school and towards the family and the parish.

Brother Gerard Rummery's *Catechesis and Religious Education in a Pluralist Society*, published in 1975, brought what had been a specialised debate on the fringes of the Catholic world into the mainstream of Catholic intellectual life.[1] Rummery's book was the first comprehensive map outlining the nature of the

---

[1] G. Rummery, *Catechesis and Religious Education in a Pluralist Society*. (Sydney: EJ Dwyer, 1975).

relationship between catechesis and Religious Education. This volume was soon followed by more focussed, albeit derivative, conceptual maps of the field of Religious Education as understood in various Christian traditions.[2]

The title of Rummery's book suggests a balanced exposé of two broad concepts. There is a laudatory Preface by Ninian Smart: this gives a clue to Rummery's overall thematic direction. An *Imprimatur* and a *Nihil Obstat*, however, seem to anchor the book firmly within the Catholic tradition. Both factors combine to give the reader a sense of anticipation at an innovative approach to reconciling insights emerging from liberal models of Religious Education with the doctrinal and educational traditions of the Catholic Church.

The keystone of Rummery's position was the need to strengthen the *educational* foundations of Religious Education. He argued that Religious Education needed a strong academic rationale in order to flourish in the school curriculum. Rummery recognised the tensions arising from the juxtaposition between *catechetical* frameworks of Religious Education and the reality of the pluralist society in which the Catholic school operated. This clearly echoes the line of thinking adopted by Smart, as we have seen. Rummery's position can be summarised as follows: catechesis is an integral part of a wider range of activities which belong to the category of Religious Education but the difference between catechesis and other forms of Religious Education is one of kind, not degree. For Rummery, educational paradigms of Religious Education are underpinned by *cognitive* and *intellectual approaches* which leave the individual free to choose religious affiliation from an informed position.

Rummery proposed the educational paradigm of Religious Education as a 'platform towards faith'. This was another way of articulating the concept of pre-evangelisation which had emerged from the International Catechetical Study Weeks and,

---

[2] Cf. K. Scott, Three Traditions of Religious Education. *Religious Education* 79 (3), 1984, pp. 323-339 and M. Boys, Religious Education: A Map of the Field. In M. Boys, Ed. *Education for Citizenship and Discipleship.* (New York: The Pilgrim Press, 1989), pp. 98-129.

interestingly, of the claims of some of the writers of early Christianity who saw a training in the classical arts as a preparation for accepting the Gospel.[3] Rummery's book hence opened Catholic intellectual life to the possibility of a renewed vision of Religious Education.

A succession of theorists developed and critiqued the line of thinking proposed by Rummery. Writing from a non-religious perspective, the British social theorist, Paul Hirst (1946-2003), wrestled with the philosophical and educational implications of how to harmonise competing religious world-views with a secular society. It is no surprise that he proposed a sharper and more rationalist edge to school-based Religious Education.[4] Hirst claimed that the ends of education are always a response to truth either as the product of natural reason or from revelation. In the clash between Revelation and reason – with reason understood as the autonomy of human knowledge – the latter will always have the upper hand. When this criterion is applied to models of religious formation, he concluded as follows: catechesis cannot be predicated on natural reason; education cannot proceed on the basis of faith (Revelation); hence there is a need to separate reason and faith, education and catechesis. The resultant model of education is, Hirst claimed, consistent with the Church's own tradition in favour of the autonomy of the disciplines.[5]

Hirst's critique of confessional approaches to Religious Education carries some intellectual weight. He rightly identified the limitations of Religious Education and broader Catholic educational approaches which fail to recognise the role of reason across the disciplines. Hirst's proposals, however, suggest that the deep-rooted suspicion towards catechetical models of Religious Education has been translated into a mistrust of the Catholic school and, indeed, any religious underpinning to education. Hirst's sharp division

---

[3] See, for example, St Clement of Alexandria, *Stromata*
[4] P. Hirst, Education, Catechesis and the Church School. *British Journal of Religious Education* 3(3), 1981, pp. 85-93.
[5] Ibid.

between reason and revelation, while helpful as an initial entry-point into the debate over the relationship between the educational and catechetical paradigms of Religious Education, ultimately serves as an exit from the Catholic tradition of faith and reason as partners in the search for truth.

The philosopher, Michael Leahy (1953-) took this debate a stage further. He argued that the use of the school classroom for purposes other than education, understood here as a critical appraisal of curriculum content, was illegitimate and, consequently, a violation of the public space of the classroom.[6] At the heart of this analysis was a philosophical rejection of insights from Revelation being transmitted within the classroom setting. Paradoxically, Leahy was open to the possibility of catechetical initiatives rooted in the wider life of the Christian school: indeed, he claimed that such initiatives should be more explicit. What is not clear in Leahy's analysis is how it is possible to reconcile a commitment to a wholly autonomous classroom within an overall school ethos which is inspired by or promotes some form of religious faith.

Alongside the ongoing philosophical re-appraisal of the roots of Religious Education and the broader division between educational and religious uses of the classroom, there was considerable thought afforded to ways in which the educational dimension of Religious Education as proposed by Rummery could be reconciled with the broader catechetical mission of the Catholic school.

The Apostolate of the Classroom

Writing during the years of the Second Vatican Council, Monsignor Eugene Kevane (1913-1996) claimed that the traditional catechetical approach to Religious Education could be contained within a sound academic setting. Kevane rejected any division between the educational work of the school and processes of religious nurture.

---

6 M. Leahy, Indoctrination, Evangelisation, Catechesis and Religious Education. *British Journal of Religious Education* 12 (3), 1991, pp. 137-144.

In *Augustine the Educator: A Study in the Fundamentals of Christian Formation*, published in 1964, Kevane held up the educational vision of St Augustine of Hippo as a model for the contemporary Church. Kevane claimed that in Augustine's vision all education was a formation in holiness; the study of the liberal arts, philosophy and theology was part of a framework which combined both study and prayer in one model of formation.[7] There are two substantial points from Kevane's comprehensive work which interestingly, show crucial lines of convergence with Rossiter.

Kevane described the teaching of religion in the Catholic school as the "apostolate of the classroom".[8] The juxtaposition of two terms which later thinkers would separate conceptually highlights the difference in approach between the more radical thinkers on the educational paradigm side of the debate and those who sought to retain a strong catechetical focus in the classroom. Kevane argued that the professional nature of the Religious Education course demanded the same degree of thoroughness as in other subjects. The subject, for Kevane, is more than a timetabled space for prayer and related pastoral activities. He argued in favour of demanding programmes of religious and spiritual formation. Unlike Rossiter, Kevane seemed more comfortable with the language of catechesis as demonstrated by his use of the terms "apostolate of the classroom" and "living catechesis" as descriptors of Religious Education.[9]

Kevane's work is wholly consonant with Catholic catechetical and educational principles. In assessing his contribution to the debate, however, it is hard to dislocate his work from the period in which it was written. Kevane was writing at a time when the practical reality for catechesis and Catholic Education was very much that of a Catholic school

---

[7] L. Franchi, St Augustine, Catechesis and Religious Education. *Religious Education* 106 (3), 2011, pp. 299-31.
[8] E. Kevane, *Augustine the Educator: A Study in the Fundamentals of Christian Formation*, 1964, p. 304.
[9] Ibid., p. 304 and p. 314.

firmly encased within the traditional home/school/parish triangle. Given that Kevane was writing in the mid 1960's, there remains a question of the suitability of this model for contemporary Catholic schools with pupils from such diverse religious backgrounds. This is not to reject his argument *qua* argument but to identify the shifts in cultural capital which differentiate the decades of the early 21st century from the middle decades of the 20th century. In short, the changing social and cultural make-up of the Catholic school population cannot be ignored in our efforts to freshen our models of Religious Education.

Kevane's work is a valuable reminder of how a traditional view of Religious Education can, from its natural home in the language and conceptual framework of catechesis, cross the border separating the so-called educational and catechetical paradigms.

Catechesis and Religious Education: A Creative Divorce

A new direction in the debate was spearheaded by Graham Rossiter (1943-) an Australian De La Salle Brother. He introduced the term "creative divorce" to describe what he regarded as a wholly desirable separation between catechesis and Religious Education.[10] In diagnosing this 'lack of fit', he concluded that a conceptual separation ("creative divorce") would allow for a more authentic catechesis and allow an academically robust Religious Education programme to make a more meaningful contribution to the catechetical mission of the school.

Rossiter's ideas remind us that the *reductio ad absurdum* of the catechetical paradigm is the loss of subject status of Religious Education, leading to its becoming solely a space for catechetical activities without an obvious academic anchor. What makes Rossiter a significant voice in the debate is his desire to construct a model of Religious Education with clear

---

[10] G. Rossiter, The Need for a Creative Divorce between Catechesis and Religious Education in Catholic Schools. *Religious Education* 77 (1), 1982, pp. 21-40.

theological and academic scaffolding. He recognised that sharp divisions between a) catechesis and the pastoral life of the Catholic school and b) Religious Education as a curriculum were artificial boundaries separating distinct but related approaches to one body of knowledge.

For Rossiter, Religious Education should show congruence between an academically credible approach and a desire to foster the emotional and affective development of young people.[11] This intellectually coherent approach made Religious Education a serious subject on the curriculum and, in consequence, a major contributor to the overall development of the pupil's religious faith.

Other Catholic thinkers, however, took a different slant. This group recognised the value of a firm educational apparatus yet saw no reason to separate this model from a commitment to faith formation. Their work offers an interesting perspective on the developing conceptual journey of Religious Education.

A Permanent Catechetical Education

While Kevane was writing *Augustine the Educator* in the early 1960's, he would have been unaware, obviously, of the intensity of future debates on the nature of Religious Education. Thomas Groome (1945-), however, recognised the fraught and delicate nature of the landscape of Religious Education.

In broad terms, Groome saw great value in the use of language of catechesis in Christian religious formation. For Groome, it is important to rediscover the traditional meaning of the key terms employed in the debate. He defines the work of Religious Education as a process which looked at the transcendent dimensions of our life on earth.[12] He suggests that any educational endeavour which enables people to engage in learning about the transcendent merits the title

---

[11] G. Rossiter, Perspectives on Change in Catholic Religious Education Since the Second Vatican Council. *Religious Education* 83 (2), 1988, pp. 264-276.
[12] Ibid., p. 22.

'Religious Education'. It is a valuable term, he claims, with *religious* pointing to its specificity in the world of religion and *education* to its commonality with wider educational principles. Christian Religious Education is Religious Education localised in the sources and practices of a specific religious community.[13]

There is much to commend in Groome's under-standing of the Christian community as an educational agent. His focus is on the broader understanding of Christian education within the Christian community. Groome seems to stop short of applying his ideas to the Catholic school and the plurality of worldviews which are present in it. This limits the full application of his often valuable insights to the subject of Religious Education in contemporary Catholic schools.

Groome accepts the classic definition of catechesis as the activity of *re-echoing* the Christian story that has been transmitted throughout history. It is an instructional activity which was experienced in the early Church as a verbal exhortation and has now fallen within the wider context of Christian formation. The focus in catechesis is on the 'Christian community' as a locus of instruction.

Groome's terminological precision challenged thinking where terms like catechesis and Religious Education had often been used interchangeably. Groome was laying out the borders of a field on which key debates would take place over the coming decades. By 2001, Groome had expanded his set of definitions to include "catechetical education" as a suitable headline for the most appropriate model of Religious Education in the Catholic school.[14] This is proposed in the context of the GDC's focus on catechesis as a form of pastoral ministry: for Groome, this is a weakness in need of

---

13 Ibid., p. 25.
14 T. Groome, Conversion, Nurture, or Both: Towards a Lifelong Catechetical Education: A Cautious Reading of the GDC. *The Living Light* 37(4), 2001.

some major conceptual reworking. [15] The basis for the reworking is a fresh understanding of evangelisation, which should now be seen as a continual process of renewal for the whole Christian community. This new direction of travel developed the traditional understanding of evangelisation as prior to catechesis and, significantly, reflected Pope Paul VI's commitment in *Evangelii Nuntiandi* to "systematic religious instruction."

Groome's principal contribution to the debate is to unify the concepts of catechesis and Religious Education into one rich process of Christian formation. [16] They are related lenses through which the heritage of Christianity is viewed, nurtured, studied and communicated. He is offering a remedy for any perceived 'irrationality' of catechesis: it is this recovery of the partnership between faith and reason which remains significant for the debate today.

Interestingly, Groome's statement that "pedagogy can be realized within a Christian community" allows him to apply a

---

[15] The GDC's cursory treatment of the value of 'instruction' as evidenced by the use of terms like "mere information" and "mere instruction" suggest a downgrading of the academic rigour which, Groome believed, was intrinsic to effective Religious Education. Cf. *General Directory for Catechesis*, 1997, 29 and 68.

[16] "During the past fifty years or so, Catholics have debated whether to use the term 'Catechesis' or 'Religious Education.' Generally, Catechesis came to mean the socialization of people into Christian identity, whereas Religious Education become more the scholarly and reflective study of a faith tradition. I worry, however, about Catechesis that shapes people's ecclesial identity without a thorough education in the whole tradition of Christian faith. On the other hand, Christian Religious Education that informs people's minds but neglects forming their identity in faith is equally troublesome. In other words, a dichotomy between these two is false and debilitating. I see them – Catechesis and Religious Education – as two essential aspects of the same endeavor. Both values – socialization and education – *must be* and with an appropriate pedagogy *can be* realized within a Christian community. This is why I use the term 'catechetical education' throughout – to emphasize the need for both" (T. Groome, *Conversion, Nurture, or Both: Towards a Lifelong Catechetical Education: A Cautious Reading of the GDC*, 2001, p. 13).

more *inductive* model to the teaching of doctrine.[17] This is a claim
that good educational principles rooted in 'reason' can be applied
to the sharing of the Christian message. In his advocacy of
educationally sound catechesis, Groome is following the lines of
argument set out by Pope Paul VI in *Evangelii Nuntiandi* and
Pope John Paul II in *Catechesi Tradendae* as well as providing a
contemporary application of Kevane's work as discussed above.
The logical conclusion to his insights on the relationship
between catechesis and Religious Education is found in the title
of his important article *Religious Education and Catechesis: No
Divorce for the Children's Sake.*[18] Groome is reinforcing both the
catechetical and the educational dimensions of Religious
Education. This is a clear response to Rossiter's earlier proposal
for a "creative divorce" in order to promote mutual enrichment
and greater effectiveness of both fields.

To summarise Groome's position, Religious Education is
catechetical in its commitment to developing faith; catechesis is
educational, as it requires study of doctrine. This accords with
previous Magisterial statements on the desirability of
systematic courses of religious instruction in the Church. To
sum up, Kevane, Rossiter and Groome are three significant
voices in the contemporary debates in the field. Together,
they have made a significant contribution to the development
of Religious Education.

The Congregation for Catholic Education has little choice
to respond to this burst of intellectual and scholarly energy.

---

[17] Groome offers his famous 'shared praxis' as a methodological channel to
lie at the heart of his favoured model of Christian Religious Education. A
full critique of this approach is beyond the scope of the present book.
[18] T. Groome, Religious Education: No Divorce for the Children's Sake,
Catholic Education 16 (4), 2007, pp. 12-14.

CHAPTER 8
RELIGIOUS EDUCATION:
THE RESPONSE OF THE MAGISTERIUM

The Magisterium responded to the fresh thinking on Religious Education in its corpus of catechetical and educational. documents. In 2009 the Magisterium made explicit the 'distinction' between catechesis and Religious Education which had been foreshadowed in the scholarly literature.

Catechesis and Religious Education: The Catechetical Documents
Church teaching on education was initially unaffected by the issues arising from the debates in academic circles on suitable conceptual frameworks of Religious Education. It seemed that such debates were encircling rather than penetrating the Magisterium. In the 1979 Apostolic Exhortation *Catechesi Tradendae*, Pope John Paul saw catechesis as a specific moment in the broader process of evangelisation.[1]

Although Pope John Paul II had written in *Catechesi Tradendae* about the role of catechesis in the school, he had not mentioned the specific *relationship* between it and Religious

---

[1] "All in all, it can be taken here that catechesis is an education of children, young people and adults in the faith, which includes especially the teaching of Christian doctrine imparted, generally speaking, in an organic and systematic way, with a view to initiating the hearers into the fullness of Christian life "(Pope John Paul II, *Catechesi Tradendae*, 1979, 18).

Education. Some recognition of a minor shift in thinking was evident in 1981 when he commented on the distinct but complementary nature of Religious Education in the school and catechesis in the parishes. [2] This intervention brought the Church into the heart of a wider academic debate which it had hitherto largely ignored as it continued to draw on catechetical theory as the dominant conceptual framework for Religious Education.

The unexpected shift in emphasis suggests that the intellectual energy arising from the debates in the wider academic world had effected some modest change in how the Church understood the role of Religious Education vis-à-vis Catechesis.

This configuration kept Religious Education at arms length from catechesis. However, Pope John Paul II also seemed to claim that Religious Education was very much linked to catechesis. [3] This implies that Religious Education would draw on the catechetical ideas either as a source of topics for study or to offer a more extensive curricular support structure. [4]

The publication of the GDC in 1997 brought together catechetical thinking in one comprehensive document. The GDC reinforced both the primacy of the parish community in

---

[2] "L'insegnamento religioso, impartito nelle scuole, e la catechesi propriamente detta, svolta nell'ambito della parrocchia, pur distinti tra loro, non devono essere considerati come separati." Author's translation: "The teaching of religion in schools and actual catechesis carried out within the parish, although distinctive, should not be considered as separate entities" (Pope John Paul, *Address to the Priests of the Diocese of Rome*, 1981, 3).

[3] "I wish to encourage you in your efforts to review Religious Education materials in order to see that they are based on principles of sound catechesis" (Pope John Paul II, *Address to the Bishops of Great Britain on the Ad Limina visit*, 1992, 6).

[4] This suggests that, in Pope John Paul II's mind at least, Religious Education was little more than an application of catechetical processes in a school setting. Such interventions are evidence of the Magisterium's developing understanding of the broader issues surrounding the question of religious nurture in the Catholic school.

catechesis and the complementarity between catechesis and Religious Education (*Religious Instruction*), stressing in particular the latter's role in cultural dialogue. For this dialogue to be fruitful, the GDC advised that the intellectual demands of Religious Education be consonant with requirements in other subjects and thus facilitate an encounter with the 'cultural patrimony' promoted by the school.[5] This position is in line with Kevane, Rossiter and Groome's espousal of the importance of fostering high academic standards in Religious Education.

The evolving relationship between evangelisation and catechesis did not leave the debate on Religious Education unaffected. [6] Religious Education's unique contribution to evangelisation seemed to lie in the teaching of a distinct body of knowledge within the school setting. While the GDC had little to say about the place of catechesis in schools, its key contribution to the debate is an affirmation of the separate conceptual frameworks of Religious Education and catechesis.[7]

This call to complementarity built on the Congregation for Catholic Education's initial definition of their distinctive identities in 1988 (see below) to ensure that there was little doubt as to their separate fields of operation. It is worth

---

[5] *General Directory for Catechesis*, 1997, endnote 22.

[6] The realignment was further enhanced by Pope Benedict XVI's Motu Proprio, *Fides per Doctrinam*, issued in 2013, which transferred competence for catechesis from the *Congregation for the Clergy* to the *Pontifical Council for Promoting New Evangelisation* "Faith needs to be strengthened through teaching, so that it can enlighten the minds and hearts of believers. The particular moment of history in which we are living, marked as it is by a dramatic crisis of faith, calls for an ability to meet the great expectations present in the hearts of believers for a response to the new questions being directed both at the world and at the Church" (Pope Benedict XVI, *Fides per Doctrinam*, Motu Proprio, 2013). This significant change could be interpreted as a call for catechesis to provide the energy for the future growth of Christianity in the 'old' Christian countries.

[7] "The relationship between religious instruction in schools and catechesis is one of distinction and complementarity: 'there is an absolute necessity to distinguish clearly between religious instruction and catechesis'" (*General Directory for Catechesis*, 1997, 73).

highlighting that the GDC itself questioned models of Religious Education which drew heavily on catechetical principles. [8] In the Magisterial documents on education, however, there is some evidence of a gradually increased awareness of the role that Religious Education plays in the wider catechetical journey of the student.

Catechesis and Religious Education: The Educational Documents
　　While the theory and practice of catechesis had been the subject of dedicated Magisterial documents, Religious Education had been considered primarily in the broader context of dedicated educational documents.

　　The Second Vatican Council had made significant shifts towards an apparent openness to the needs and anxieties of the age. To what extent did this influence thinking on education?

　　The short conciliar document on education, *Gravissimum Educationis*, while aligning itself with the broader reform agenda of the Council, drew heavily on Pope Pius XI's encyclical of 1929. [9] *Gravissimum Educationis* offered a broad focus on the principles of education and hence recognised and accepted the changing social and cultural reality of the post-war world. This cautious engagement with educational reform is encapsulated in the call for a 'special post-conciliar commission' with the specific remit to develop the notion of 'Christian education. [10] Nonetheless, *Gravissimum Educationis* would act as a charter for the evolution of Catholic thinking on education despite its reliance on a document by Pope Pius XI which seemed to be at odds with the Second Vatican Council's hope for an accommodation with the modern world. Given this broader context, it is no surprise that *Gravissimum Educationis* did not refer at all to the nature of the relationship between catechesis and education: the 'debate' had yet to begin.

---

[8] Ibid.
[9] Indeed *Gravissimum Educationis* refers to Pope Pius XI's encyclical in twelve of its thirty six footnotes.
[10] Second Vatican Council, *Gravissimum Educationis*, 1965, 65.

Although the GCD of 1971 had opted in to the broad Conciliar reforms in catechesis, it was some time before the Congregation for Catholic Education's documents began to engage with the need to consider reform in schools. The publication of *The Catholic School* in 1977 signalled the beginning of a faint change of direction in the tone of the debate in its advocacy of "catechetical instruction" in Catholic schools.[11]

The articulation of the place of the family and the wider community in religious formations was a recalling of the catechetical arrangement of early Christianity. The emphasis on catechetical instruction in the Catholic school could be interpreted as either an affirmation of a traditional 'catechesis in the classroom model' of Religious Education or, perhaps, a recognition of the need for catechetical instruction – possibly for the Sacraments of Initiation – outside the standard timetable.

Whatever the intention, the tone of the document is urgent, possibly owing to a perception that the catechetical renewal and broader educational reforms were having a detrimental effect on the transmission of doctrine. Following this document, *Lay Catholics in Schools: Witnesses to Faith*, published in 1982, turned the Church's attention to the increasingly important role of the lay (Catholic) teacher. Given the decline in the numbers of Religious from apostolic congregations and orders with a dedicated charism for education, the Church had to ensure that the growing corps of lay teachers were well formed doctrinally and pastorally. The integration of the pastoral and the academic dimension of education provided a helpful context for further development of the relationship between catechesis and Religious Education in the professional activity of the (lay) Catholic teacher.[12]

---

[11] "It is recognised that the proper place for catechesis is the family helped by other Christian communities, especially the local parish. But the importance and need for catechetical instruction in Catholic schools cannot be sufficiently emphasised. Here young people are helped to grow towards maturity in faith" (*The Catholic School*, 1977, 51).

[12] This document was the application to education and the profession of

The first major exploration of the relationship between catechesis and Religious Education in a Magisterial document comes with the publication in 1988 of *The Religious Dimension of Education in a Catholic School.*[13] What makes this document highly influential is its clear articulation for the first time in a Magisterial document of the *distinctive* and *complementary* spheres of influence of catechesis and Religious Education.[14] This new position reflects both Rossiter's notion of separate but adjacent fields of operation for Catechesis and Religious Education as well as Pope John Paul II's view of Religious Education as a space for reflection on the content of

---

teaching of the principles of the lay apostolate which had been laid out by the Second Vatican Council in *Apostolicam Actuositatem.* This second part of the educational trilogy focused on the promotion of a distinctive Catholic identity rooted in the synthesis of faith, culture and life. See pp. 29-31.

[13] The broad theme of this substantial document is that all education has a religious dimension and within this theme there is a major exposition of the aims and principles of Catholic Education, an analysis of which is beyond the scope of the present book.

[14] "There is a close connection, and at the same time a clear distinction, between religious instruction and catechesis, or the handing on of the Gospel message. The close connection makes it possible for a school to remain a school and still integrate culture with the message of Christianity. The distinction comes from the fact that, unlike religious instruction, catechesis presupposes that the hearer is receiving the Christian message as a salvific reality. Moreover, catechesis takes place within a community living out its faith at a level of space and time not available to a school: a whole lifetime. The aim of catechesis, or handing on the Gospel message, is maturity: spiritual, liturgical, sacramental and apostolic; this happens most especially in a local Church community. The aim of the school, however, is knowledge. While it uses the same elements of the Gospel message, it tries to convey a sense of the nature of Christianity, and of how Christians are trying to live their lives. It is evident, of course, that religious instruction cannot help but strengthen the faith of a believing student, just as catechesis cannot help but increase one's knowledge of the Christian message. The distinction between religious instruction and catechesis does not change the fact that a school can and must play its specific role in the work of catechesis. Since its educational goals are rooted in Christian principles, the school as a whole is inserted into the evangelical function of the Church. It assists in and promotes faith education" (*The Religious Dimension of Education in the Catholic School,* 1988, 67-68).

Catechesis. It rejects sharp conceptual separations while holding on to a degree of separateness in order to avoid a merging of the disciplines of catechesis and Religious Education.

Paragraphs 67-68 reveal that the perceived *dichotomy* between catechesis and Religious Education, which had been the subject of much scholarly writing in the early 1980's, had been finally recognised by the Magisterium as an authentic expression of the Catholic 'mind' on education. This configuration encouraged the development of a strong academic rationale for Religious Education in its advocacy of a strong scholastic framework which should include an approved syllabus, inter-disciplinary links and, when possible, public examinations.

This is further evidence of the strengthening of the *educational* model of Religious Education in the light of the insights gathered from the wider field of educational studies *viz* objectives, syllabus and methodology. The Religious Education curriculum is not, however, a derivative or second-rate catechesis but a body of knowledge with its unique way of analysing culture and the human condition. The school is hence accorded a unique status as a place of intense dialogue between Christianity and 'the world', a position wholly in keeping with the teaching of the Second Vatican Council.[15] catechesis. Given the advances in scholarship, it was necessary to produce further focussed guidance on nature of the subject.

Catechesis and Religious Education: The Circular Letter of 2009
The lack of clear direction in the Magisterial teaching of the Church on the concrete nature and curricular shape of the

---

[15] A second concern is the place of *Other World Religions* in the Religious Education class. Although this dimension of Religious Education is underpinned by knowledge and not explicit faith formation, it is taken for granted in the Magisterial documents that the Catholic school will have the teaching of Christianity as its fundamental point of reference. There is little recognition of the place of *Other World Religions* and other ways of thinking in this approach. This leaves the Church open to accusations, whether just or unjust, of a religious exclusivism at variance with the modern and wholly desirable vision of the school as a place of encounter with the 'other'.

subject of Religious Education is problematic when set against the thorough Magisterial treatment of catechesis as evidenced by the publication of two *Directories* related to catechesis since the Second Vatican Council.

The *Circular Letter to the Presidents of Bishops' Conferences on Religious Education in Schools* in 2009 (henceforth *Circular Letter)* was a ground-breaking, if inadequately reported, initiative. Although the *Circular Letter* is a short document, its status as the first pronouncement by the Congregation for Catholic Education on Religious Education makes it a key resource for developments in the field.

The *Circular Letter* articulates the key ideas which had been developed across a range of other documents on both catechesis and education.[16] As an initial 'charter' for Religious Education, it allows the Church's teaching to be more accessible, increases the status of the subject and, hopefully, works against its misrepresentation as an explicitly catechetical endeavour in a school setting.

The *Circular Letter* presents the relationship between catechesis and Religious Education in very plain terms. Those unaware of the antecedents of this document would be in danger of interpreting it as a denial of the Catholic school's role in the faith formation of the pupils.[17] Dealing with the specific question of the broader school curriculum, the *Circular Letter* calls Religious Education an essential element in the life of the school: it plays a role in the evangelising mission of the Church and complements the broader catechetical initiatives in the family and the parish.[18]

---

[16] Cf. *The Religious Dimension of Education in the Catholic School*, 1988 and the *General Directory for Catechesis*, 1997.

[17] Note the implied distinction between catechesis and Religious Education in schools in Pope Benedict's Address to the Bishops of Australia: "All the members of the Church need to be formed in their faith, from a sound catechesis for children, and Religious Education imparted in your Catholic schools, to much-needed catechetical programmes for adults" (See Pope Benedict XVI, *Ad Limina to the Australian Bishops*, 2011).

[18] "Catechesis aims at fostering personal adherence to Christ and the development of Christian life in its different aspects whereas Religious

So what is going on here? It seems that the arguments advanced by Rossiter for a "creative divorce" have been accepted by the Magisterium yet the closeness of the new relationship shows that Groome's advocacy of "no divorce" has also been influential. This would suggest that the Church is looking for inspiration from more than one intellectual position and is still seeking ways of developing and concretising the complex relationship. While this openness to scholarship and intellectual life is welcome, is it the case that those responsible for the design of programmes of Religious Education, for now, lack a clear conceptual template?

Looking Ahead

The Magisterium has responded to changes in the landscape of Religious Education and allowed its own traditional catechetical approach to Religious Education to be influenced by some new thinking. Of course, the Congregation for Catholic Education could have resisted this call to reform and retained a strict catechetical paradigm within the school as a theological safety barrier against the advance of secularist ideas. The fact that this did not happen is a significant indicator of openness to new ideas.

The gradual embrace of the educational paradigm reflected the (perennial) call to enter into dialogue with other ways of thinking. It recalled the early years of the Catechetical reform movement, with its embrace of insights into processes of learning culminating in the systematic planning which lay at the heart of the Munich method. Hence, the Magisterium was, once again, looking around at developments in the wider world of ideas and assessing whether, and to what extent, they could enhance its own ways of thinking.

The emphasis on a harmonious relationship between catechesis and Religious Education gives the lie to any claim that a commitment to an *educational paradigm* precludes any

---

Education in schools gives the pupils knowledge about Christianity's identity and Christian life" (*Circular Letter to Presidents of Bishops' Conferences on Religious Education in Schools*, 2009, 17).

aspiration to faith commitment or faith nurture in the Catholic school curriculum.[19]

On the other hand, a separation between Religious Education and the broader faith formation of the pupil might be at variance with the Catholic school's broader mission to participate in evangelisation. If evangelisation is central to the total experience of the school community, there must be limited space for activities which are not part of the mission to evangelise.

Owing to the impact of these issues on pastoral and theological dimensions of Catholic life, they need addressing in a context wider than is provided by the fields of catechesis, education and Religious Education alone. Only a deeper and theologically-driven investigation of the relationship between catechesis and Religious Education will allow a satisfactory response to the issues mentioned above. In Part 3 we consider how the theological model of the Church as communion (*communio*)can strengthen the relationship between catechesis and Religious Education.

---

[19] This is similar to the sentiments expressed by Pope Benedict XVI in the *Address to the Catholic Religion Teachers*, 2009, where he makes the Christian case for the unity of religious and human formation.

PART 3
CATECHESIS AND RELIGIOUS EDUCATION: A SPIRITUALITY OF COMMUNION

The notion of unity-in-diversity, a key feature of the theology of *communio*, offers a viable hermeneutic for a renewed and richer understanding of the relationship between catechesis and Religious Education. To understand the breadth and depth of this term, we examine the notion of *communio* in the context of tradition and progress. Only then is it possible to glimpse the richness of *communio* as a interpretive key and make sense of Pope John Paul II's use of the term "spirituality of communion", as the underpinning principle of all formational activities.[1] In keeping with the notion of *unity-in-diversity*, Pope John Paul II describes it as a way of making room for and recognising what is positive in others and welcoming the other as a gift from God. This suggests strongly that *communio* is more than an just another ecclesiological model but is, in reality, a dynamic force which underpins and shapes the wider life of the Christian. This argument is set out as follows:

- What does *communio* mean as a theological expression (Chapter 9)?
- What is understood by the term 'Spirituality of Communion' (Chapter 10)?
- How can Shared Mission bring together catechesis and Religious Education (Chapter 11)?

---

[1] Pope John Paul II, *Novo Millennio Ineunte*, 43.

CHAPTER 9
EXPLORING *COMMUNIO*

In the opening address to the delegates assembled for the Second Vatican Council, Pope John XXIII spoke of both *tradition* and *progress* as key constituents of the Church's role in the modern world. [1] What did he mean by this choice of words? Essentially, Pope John was outlining a vision of the Council as the latest stage in the Church's "uninterrupted witness." He fully understood the need to develop new ways of teaching and giving witness to the modern world while retaining the "sacred patrimony of truth inherited from the Fathers", yet recognising the "changing conditions of the modern world." He wanted the Church's body of doctrine ('sacred patrimony of truth') to be preserved while ensuring that the Church was not regarded as an institution concerned exclusively with preservation of historical traditions for their own sake.

This call for change reflected Cardinal John Henry Newman's criteria for assessing whether doctrinal developments were authentic or simply the grafting of new ideas onto the Christian worldview. To be sure, all developments in doctrine, if they are to be legitimate, must grow from already established doctrinal traditions.[2] What is remarkable in Pope John XXIII's

---

[1] Pope John XXIII, Opening Address to the Second Vatican Council, 1962.

[2] JH. Newman, *An Essay on the Development of Christian Doctrine*, 1878/2003.

opening address is the sense of historical, theological and pastoral perspective he brings to the table. Alongside the call to conservation of Tradition, he emphasised the need to be aware of the demands arising from social and cultural changes in the world. Pope John thus offered scope for some form of innovation in the Church's mode of engagement with such forces: the call to conserve Tradition was not a summons to retreat behind the walls of a fossilised theological tradition.

The Second Vatican Council itself had offered an example of how the *tradition/progress* relationship could effect substantial reform across many aspects of Catholic life. The Council revolved around the twin axes of *ressourcement* and *aggiornamento* and the fruit of its deliberations was a set of documents which made, and continue to make, a deep impact on contemporary Catholic life.[3]

In the years during and following the Second Vatican Council, ancient terms like People of God and *communio* were recovered from the worlds of Judaism and early Christianity and reconsidered in the broad context of the *tradition/progress* relationship. The theology of *communio* had much to offer Catholic thought at an important juncture in its history. It was the re-discovery of the value for the contemporary Church of an ancient Christian term (*koinonia* – fellowship) and hence reflected the intersection of the twin themes of *ressourcement* and *aggiornamento*.[4]

---

[3] A good example of this dialectic is found in the Second Vatican Council's *Perfectae Caritas: Decree on the Adaptation and Renewal of Religious Life*. It captured the dynamic relationship between the need to reserve tradition yet find ways in which the energy of the original charism of the order could provide a fund of restorative energy. "The adaptation and renewal of the religious life includes both the constant return to the sources of all Christian life and to the original spirit of the institutes and their adaptation to the changed conditions of our time" (*Perfectae Caritatis*, 1965, 2).

[4] The re-emergence of *communio* as an ecclesiological paradigm (or category) was part of the Catholic Intellectual Revival of the late nineteenth and early twentieth century. The work of the Dominican, Yves Congar (1904-1995) and the Jesuit, Henri de Lubac (1896-1991), were instrumental in the recovery of the early Church's focus on *koinonia*, and offer it, suitably

Communio offered a rich and nuanced vision of the Church. It harmonised the necessary mystical and spiritual underpinning of Catholic ecclesiology with the concrete reality of people on a long and often arduous journey of faith.[5] Furthermore, the apparently wide parameters of *communio* was a shield against particularist, or exclusivist, interpretations of existing models of the Church lacking in any semblance of historical and theological subtlety. This was another step away from the political-society model of ecclesiology which had predominated in the late nineteenth century.[6]

The concept of *communio* is bound to the sacramental traditions of the Church: in Catholic teaching, sacramental communion is the source of, and inspiration for, Christian unity and Christian living.[7] The Pauline image of the Church as the Mystical Body of Christ reflects the vitality of the Trinity of Father, Son and Spirit. *Communio*, properly understood, allows for grace-filled participation in the life of the Church.

The re-emergence of *communio* in the mainstream of

---

refreshed, as a model of Church suitable for the modern age. See for example, H. De Lubac, *The Splendor of the Church.* (San Francisco: Ignatius Press, 1956/1986) and Y. Congar, *Diversity and Communion.* (New London: Twenty-third Publications, 1985) for examples of how this Catholic intellectual revival informed thinking in ecclesiology.

[5] Reflection on *communio* offers an image of unity in diversity/diversity in unity which flows from consideration of the nature of the Trinity. Despite the apparent strengths of the model, the question of unity in diversity/ diversity in unity remains ecclesiologically problematic. While 'unity in diversity' surely reflects the pastoral intentions of the Conciliar and post-Conciliar documents and offers some scope for outreach and inclusion, matters of Catholic teaching have, by definition, fixed outposts. There is clearly a limit to the diversity of belief and expression which can sit comfortably within any unified body of doctrine.

[6] For essential reading on models of ecclesiology, see A. Dulles, *Models of the Church.* (New York: Doubleday, 2002.)

[7] The *Didache* (ch. 9) and the *First Apology of St Justin the Martyr* are possible eyewitness (or participant) accounts of early Christian worship. The latter's account has been included into the text of the *Catechism of the Catholic Church* in paragraph 1345.

Catholic life broadened the theological basis of ecclesiology. While the image of the Church as the Mystical Body of Christ was shaped principally by images drawn from Christology, *communio* retained the language of sacramentality while offering theological underpinning from the doctrine of the Trinity.[8]

This allowed the aspect of relationship and dynamism, intrinsic to the theology of Trinity, to influence ecclesiological thought.[9] It opened Catholic teaching to new ways of understanding the respective role of the priest and lay person and, crucially, encouraged Catholic Christianity to enter into deeper dialogue with Christian communities not *in communion* with the Holy See.[10] Here are discerned the seeds of later

---

[8] "The divine persons are relative to one another. Because it does not divide the divine unity, the real distinction of the persons from one another resides solely in the relationships which relate them to one another" (CCC, 235).

[9] Avery Dulles sketches out the ecclesiological ideas of Pope John Paul II in Appendix 1 of *Models of the Church* (2002). This essay is a helpful introduction to the place of *communio* in the life of the Church.

[10] "Even in the beginnings of this one and only Church of God there arose certain rifts, which the Apostle strongly condemned. But in subsequent centuries much more serious dissensions made their appearance and quite large communities came to be separated from full communion with the Catholic Church – for which, often enough, men of both sides were to blame. The children who are born into these Communities and who grow up believing in Christ, cannot be accused of the sin involved in the separation, and the Catholic Church embraces upon (sic) them as brothers, with respect and affection. For men who believe in Christ and have been truly baptized are in communion with the Catholic Church even though this communion is imperfect. The differences that exist in varying degrees between them and the Catholic Church – whether in doctrine and sometimes in discipline, or concerning the structure of the Church – do indeed create many obstacles, sometimes serious ones, to full ecclesiastical communion. The ecumenical movement is striving to overcome these obstacles. But even in spite of them it remains true that all who have been justified by faith in Baptism are members of Christ's body, and have a right to be called Christian, and so are correctly accepted as brothers by the children of the Catholic Church. Moreover, some and even very many of the significant elements and endowments which together go to build up and give life to the Church itself, can exist outside the visible boundaries of the Catholic Church: the written word of God; the life of grace; faith, hope

ecumenical initiatives which would revolve around applying *communio* to concrete pastoral situations with the Anglican communion and the Orthodox Church.[11]

The *Extraordinary Synod of Bishops* in 1985 reassessed the nature of the Church in the light of post-Conciliar developments. In a sense it acted as "balance sheet for the twenty years of the Council".[12] With regard to the images (or models) of Church which had emerged from the Council, the 1985 Synod, crucially, put *communio* at the heart of its thinking.[13] This development marked the early stages of the journey of *communio* to become more than another ecclesiological model: *Communio* was now a prism through which other themes could be interpreted.

The value of *communio* as a hermeneutical key was further stressed in 1992 with the publication of *Communionis noto* – a Letter to the Bishops of the Church from the Congregation for the Doctrine of the Faith. The purpose of *Communionis noto* was to restore some balance to debates on the nature of the Church, a sign perhaps that the proposals of the 1985 Extraordinary Synod had not made a significant impact on Catholic thinking on ecclesiology.

In this Letter, the focus on *communio* in the 1985 Extraordinary Synod is revisited owing to a perceived lack of

---

and charity, with the other interior gifts of the Holy Spirit, and visible elements too. All of these, which come from Christ and lead back to Christ, belong by right to the one Church of Christ" (Second Vatican Council, *Unitas Redintegratio*, 1964, 3).

[11] See the following documents: Second Anglican/Roman Catholic International Commission (*ARCIC II*) *The Church as Communion*, 1991, especially paragraph 2; the Joint International Commission for the Theological Dialogue between the Roman Catholic Church and the Orthodox Church – better known as the *Ravenna Document*, 2007.

[12] J. Ratzinger, *Pilgrim Fellowship of Faith: The Church as Communion*. (San Francisco: Ignatius Press, 2005), p. 129.

[13] "...the Church is sacrament, that is, sign and instrument of communion with God and also of communion and reconciliation of men with one another. The message of the Church, as described in the Second Vatican Council, is Trinitarian and Christocentric" (Second Extraordinary Synod *The Church, in the Word of God, Celebrates the Mysteries of Christ*, 1985, 2.)

integration in Church life between ecclesiological models such as People of God and Body of Christ. This was a matter of general doctrinal and pastoral importance.[14] *Communionis noto* is rooted in and reflects on earlier teachings of the Magisterium, in particular, the teachings of the Second Vatican Council.[15] As such, it serves as a clear indication of how the Church understands *communio* as a *hermeneutic of unity* which offers avenues for future theological investigation.

Communio challenges any sense of compartmentalisation

---

[14] *Communionis noto*'s key point is the precedence of the universal Church over the local, or particular Church. "The universal Church is therefore the *Body of the Churches*. Hence it is possible to apply the concept of communion *in analogous fashion* to the union existing among particular Churches, and to see the universal Church as a *Communion of Churches*. Sometimes, however, the idea of a 'communion of particular Churches' is presented in such a way as to weaken the concept of the unity of the Church at the visible and institutional level. Thus it is asserted that every particular Church is a subject complete in itself, and that the universal Church is the result of a *reciprocal recognition* on the part of the particular Churches. This ecclesiological unilateralism, which impoverishes not only the concept of the universal Church but also that of the particular Church, betrays an insufficient understanding of the concept of communion. As history shows, when a particular Church has sought to become self-sufficient, and has weakened its real communion with the universal Church and with its living and visible centre, its internal unity suffers too, and it finds itself in danger of losing its own freedom in the face of the various forces of slavery and exploitation. In order to grasp the true meaning of the analogical application of the term *communion* to the particular Churches taken as a whole, one must bear in mind above all that the particular Churches, insofar as they are *'part of the one Church of Christ'*, have a special relationship of *'mutual interiority'* with the whole, that is, with the universal Church, because in every particular Church *'the one, holy, catholic and apostolic Church of Christ is truly present and active'*. For this reason, *'the universal Church cannot be conceived as the sum of the particular Churches, or as a federation of particular Churches'*. It is not the result of the communion of the Churches, but, in its essential mystery, it is a reality *ontologically and temporally* prior to every *individual* particular Church" (*Communionis Noto*, 8-9).

[15] The section headings of the document are helpful as signposts to the principal themes in contemporary ecclesiology: The Church, a Mystery of Communion; Universal Church and Particular Churches; Communion of the Churches, Eucharist and Episcopate; Unity and Diversity in Ecclesial Communion; Ecclesial Communion and Ecumenism.

of doctrine: Trinity, Christology, sacramental theology and ecclesiology, for example, are bound together as expressions of the dynamism of the Church's patrimony. It hence provides the theological architecture which allows catechesis and Religious Education to enjoy a common language of faith while respecting their differing modes of operation.

In this context, the shared language of faith allows the Catholic school to become a place of evangelisation where the educational experience is informed by Catholic culture.[16] The relationship between *communio* and the Catholic school finds expression in a vision of the Catholic school animated by its distinct ecclesial nature.[17] In this vision of education, the Catholic school is a Trinitarian and Christocentric community of faith where all are encouraged to live according to the Gospel. The alignment between the mission of the Church and the life, work and educational goals of the Catholic school comes from the mutual and historically-conditioned reciprocity between Church and school.

This model of Catholic Education is dependent on the continued existence of committed and well-formed teachers who are instrumental in shaping the vision and the mission of the Catholic school. The important notion of Spiritual Capital – the array of faith, traditions and values which have emerged from the Catholic Christian tradition – acquired by key staff in Catholic schools allows these staff to serve as both good professionals and authentic witnesses in the school.[18] The Spiritual Capital at the heart of the institution ensures that the Catholic school is shaped by a distinctive faith-based vision of education.[19]

What does all this mean for the Catholic school in a pluralist society? The nature of the dialogue between the

---

[16] *The Catholic School on the Threshold of the Third Millennium,* 11-14.

[17] *The Religious Dimension of Education in a Catholic School, passim*

[18] G. Grace, *Catholic Schools: Mission, Markets, Morality.* (London: Routledge Farmer, 2002).

[19] See S. McKinney (Ed.), *Faith Schools in the Twenty-first Century.* (Edinburgh: Dunedin Academic Press Ltd, 2008) for a succinct overview of key issues re 'faith-schools' in a plural society.

Church and public authorities on the provision of Catholic school education is crucial. This dialogue can be on two levels. First, it can be a politically-inspired process which defends the right of Catholic schools to exist within a pluralist educational system. Second, the dialogue can focus on how the Church's rich educational heritage can make a positive contribution to public debates on the nature and purpose of schooling. In the latter model, the Catholic school acts out the politically sensitive role of offering a distinctive vision of education which simultaneously offers philosophical challenges to the foundations of the pluralist society itself.

This model of the Catholic school promotes an integral vision of academic learning and human formation which eschews a narrow focus on academic success or on any other performative indicator. Pope Benedict XVI's reflections on the so-called "educational emergency" articulate a way of thinking which is concerned with broader educational issues – in this case the challenge to the exercise of legitimate authority and norms of behaviour in society, and not solely with matters concerning the working of the Catholic system.[20]

This model of the Catholic school is an innovative way of engaging the Catholic school with contemporary life and gives a radical edge to the Catholic school's relationship with both the state and the surrounding culture. The theology of *communio* places the Catholic school at the intersection between the Church's worldview and the necessary responsibility of the state to oversee education systems. Within this context, the Catholic school's philosophy is one which seeks to harmonise aspects of *communio* with the mission to educate.[21] The

---

[20] Pope Benedict XVI's address to the assembly of the Diocese of Rome in 2007 contained a profound concern arising from developments in modern educational thought which were, he believed, inimical to the development of truly human values. See Pope Benedict XVI, *Address to the Participants in the Convention of the Diocese of Rome, 2007*.

[21] "On the other hand, because of its identity and its ecclesial roots, this community must aspire to becoming a Christian community, that is, a community of faith, able to create increasingly more profound relations of

Church's intellectual heritage overflows into the Catholic school's relations with wider society. The resultant synthesis of faith and culture challenges the settled pluralism of contemporary education as it promotes an educational programme coherent with the Catholic worldview. This assists the development of a wisdom which, to a greater or lesser extent, opens pupils' horizons and gladdens hearts.[22]

communion which are themselves educational. It is precisely the presence and life of an educational community, in which all the members participate in a fraternal communion, nourished by a living relationship with Christ and with the Church, that makes the Catholic school the environment for an authentically ecclesial experience" (*Educating Together in Catholic Schools: A Shared Mission between Consecrated Persons and the Lay Faithful.* 2007, 14).

[22] For more on this, see S. Caldecott, *Beauty in the Word: Rethinking the Foundations of Education.* (Tacoma: Angelico Press, 2012).

CHAPTER 10
THE SPIRITUALITY OF COMMUNION:
TOWARDS A SHARED MISSION

A Spirituality of Communion, understood as the guiding principle of all formational processes, locates Catholic Education firmly within the Church's broader evangelising mission yet leaves space for the legitimate diversity which lies at the heart of *communio*. A partner term, Integral Religious Formation, provides a robust underpinning for the developing relationship between catechesis and Religious Education within the theological architecture provided by *communio*.

Spirituality of Communion: A Hermeneutical Key for Catholic Education
The Catholic school is called to be an educational community which forms the human person in integral unity and hence supports the formation of bonds of communion. Pope John Paul II's proposal for a Spirituality of Communion hence offers an interpretive, or hermeneutical key, for understanding more fully the relationship between catechesis and Religious Education. [1] The emphasis on the Trinity

---

[1] "Before making practical plans, we need to promote a spirituality of communion, making it the guiding principle of education wherever individuals and Christians are formed, wherever ministers of the altar, consecrated persons, and pastoral workers are trained, wherever families and communities are being built up. A spirituality of communion indicates above all the heart's contemplation of the mystery of the Trinity dwelling in us, and whose light we must also be able to see shining on the face of the brothers and sisters

illustrates the links between theology and the principles, processes and loci of education. It reveals how theological knowledge of the mystery of the Trinity can be applied to all expressions of Christian life. The relationship between catechesis and Religious Education follows on from the Church's gradual absorption of the implications of *communio* for wider Catholic life and identity.

Such intellectual and pastoral currents had a profound influence on the Church's thinking on catechesis. As previously noted, the GCD of 1971 had drawn on the Second Vatican Council and the fruits of Catholic theological scholarship to make initial links between the Church as *communio* and the field of catechesis.[2] This influence, implicit at first, grew in importance in parallel with ongoing reflection on the implications of *communio* for contemporary Catholic life. The Magisterial documents now began to consider seriously how *communio* had the theological potential to reshape thinking

---

around us. A spirituality of communion also means an ability to think of our brothers and sisters in faith within the profound unity of the Mystical Body, and therefore as 'those who are a part of me'. This makes us able to share their joys and sufferings, to sense their desires and attend to their needs, to offer them deep and genuine friendship. A spirituality of communion implies also the ability to see what is positive in others, to welcome it and prize it as a gift from God: not only as a gift for the brother or sister who has received it directly, but also as a 'gift for me'. A spirituality of communion means, finally, to know how to 'make room' for our brothers and sisters, bearing 'each other's burdens' (Gal 6:2) and resisting the selfish temptations which constantly beset us and provoke competition, careerism, distrust and jealousy. Let us have no illusions: unless we follow this spiritual path, external structures of communion will serve very little purpose. They would become mechanisms without a soul, 'masks' of communion rather than its means of expression and growth" (Pope John Paul II, *Novo Millennio Ineunte*, 43.)

2 "The Church is a communion. She herself acquired a fuller awareness of that truth in the Second Vatican Council. The Church is a people assembled by God and united by close spiritual bonds. Her structure needs a diversity of gifts and offices; and yet the distinctions within them, though they can be not only of degree but also of essence, as is the case between the ministerial priesthood and the common priesthood of the people, by no means takes away the basic and essential equality of persons" (*General Catechetical Directory*, 1971, 66).

on Catholic Education.

An exploration of the key Magisterial teaching in this field reveal the growing importance of the relationship between *communio* and education. This came to maturation with the publication of *Educating Together in Catholic Schools – A Shared Mission between Consecrated Person and the Lay Faithful*, published in 2007. The importance of this document goes beyond the mere exploration of the relationship between the lay teacher and the teacher from a Religious Order.[3] *Educating Together* finally made explicit the thematic links between *communio* and education which had been largely implicit in Church teaching since the early 1970's.[4] It applies the key aspects of *communio* to Catholic Education and hence was as an important thematic bridge between theological reflection on *communio* and Catholic teaching on education.[5]

A crucial feature of *Educating Together* is its description of Catholic Education as founded on a "shared mission".[6] As discussed in Chapter Three, John Baptiste De La Salle had introduced Religious Brothers as teachers in seventeenth century France. The growth of other orders and congregations with an interest in education widened the Catholic teaching

---

[3] *Lay Catholics in School: Witnesses to Faith*, 1982 and *Consecrated Persons and their Mission in Schools*, 2002, although separated by a period of twenty years, are partner documents which deal with these issues in some detail.

[4] Cf. *Lay Catholics in Schools: Witnesses to Faith*, 18, 28; *The Religious Dimension of Education in a Catholic School*, 44, 81; *The Catholic School on the Threshold of the Third Millennium*: 11-13, 18; *Consecrated Persons and their Mission in Schools*, 15. *Educating Together in Catholic Schools*, 2007, offers a summary of the important themes of *communio*: the *essence* of the Church and the Church as *icon* of the love of God.

[5] *Educating Together in Catholic Schools*, 2007, 8-19.

[6] Ibid., 5: "The implementation of a real *educational community*, built on the foundation of shared mission and values, represents a serious task that must be carried out by the Catholic school. In this setting, the presence both of students and of teachers from different cultural and religious backgrounds requires an increased commitment of discernment and accompaniment. The preparation of a shared mission acts as a stimulus that should force the Catholic school to be a place of ecclesial experience."

force beyond the priesthood.[7] In the Magisterial documents, the Shared Mission emerged in response to a drop in vocations to Religious orders/congregations with a charism for teaching. Shared Mission is thus used retrospectively to describe a situation which had arisen from the decline in vocations to dedicated teaching orders/congregations.

A case could be made that the use of Shared Mission in this case is no more than a necessary and limited intervention in response to the changing demographic of the teaching force. The altered demography of the teaching force in Catholic schools has allowed the Church to re-conceptualise the role of the lay teacher. However, this is not the full story as it offered an opportunity for the Church to appreciate in greater depth the growing participation of lay people in teaching. Shared Mission is an example of the Spirituality of Communion as applied to education. The Church's acceptance of the principle of a Shared Mission between the lay teacher and the teacher from a Religious order/congregation leaves open the possibility of other ways of understanding the term.

Religious Education: A Shared Mission

How satisfactory is Shared Mission as a descriptor of the relationship between catechesis and Religious Education? Before going any further, it is necessary to clarify precisely what is understood by this term.

Shared Mission in this context recognises the contribution of the different participants in the project of Catholic Education: the parish, the school, Bishops' Conferences and associated Church agencies. The family, of course remains the irreplaceable influence. Furthermore, Catholic Education in most modern settings cannot ignore the

---

[7] Cf. T. O'Donoghue, *Come Follow Me and Forsake Temptation: Catholic Schooling and the Retention of Teachers for Religious Teaching Orders, 1922-1965.* (Berne: Peter Lang, 2004); *Catholic Teaching Brothers: Their Life in the English-Speaking World 1891-1965.* (New York: Palgrave Macmillan, 2012); B. Hellinckx, F. Simon and M. Depaepe, *The Forgotten Contribution of the Teaching Sisters.* (Leuven: Leuven University Press, 2009).

role of the state, especially where the state is a lead provider and funder of education.

Additionally, Shared Mission identifies Religious Education as having roots in both catechesis and much broader educational influences (see Chapter Three). This is in line with the claim of the Magisterium that catechesis and Religious Education are complementary processes. The Magisterium has not suggested how the complementarity could be encouraged, far less achieved. The evolution of Religious Education from 'school-based catechesis' to full academic subject status hence remains a work in progress. Nonetheless, reflection on *communio* teases out the principles of the Shared Mission and helps to identify some points of *consonance* and *dissonance* between both fields.

Areas of Consonance between Catechesis and Religious Education

Religious Education shares a body of doctrine with catechesis. In the Catholic school, this body of knowledge should be taught systematically. [8] This arrangement is a reflection of the subject's roots in catechesis and of the critical engagement with culture which contemporary understandings of Religious Education are designed to promote.

The Church's deposit of faith aligns the Catholic school with the broader life and mission of the Church. Religious Education, as a *complement* to catechesis, thereby presupposes some form of supportive family/parish structures.[9]

The knowledge and understanding which lie at the heart of Religious Education is the fruit of study and personal reflection on the Church's doctrinal heritage.[10] Furthermore, the Church also claims that "there is no separation between time for learning and time for formation, between acquiring

---

[8] Compare Pope Pius X, *Acerbo Nimis*, 1905, 4 and *The Catholic School on the Threshold of the Third Millennium*, 1997, 851 for statements from both ends of the twentieth century on the importance of teaching doctrine satisfactorily.
[9] *General Directory for Catechesis*, 1997, 225-231.
[10] Ibid., 154.

notions and growing in wisdom." [11] For example, while memorisation is a key component of developing knowledge and understanding, any texts committed to memory are more than providers of religious data: they serve as the primary material on which the student can apply a wide range of pedagogical tools.[12]

Religious Education is, therefore, a legitimate *development* of catechesis in the context of the Catholic school. The question of what is understood by 'legitimate development' is crucial to understanding the Shared Mission. Cardinal Newman argued that Christian doctrine could not remain a static and unchanging body of knowledge as these bodies of knowledge grew throughout history. What makes this a process of development, as opposed to one of corruption, of earlier ideas is, he argued, the clear continuity between the later and earlier stages of development. [13] Although Newman was concerned with demonstrating doctrinal continuity between the early (apostolic) Church and the Catholic Church of the nineteenth century, the principles he enunciated can be applied to the relationship between catechesis and Religious Education today.

The proposal that Religious Education is a legitimate development of catechesis accords with the Newmanian notion that all developments in Church teaching must have clear roots in (and be implicit in) what went before. The distinction is crucial given the claim above that catechesis shares a body of knowledge with Religious Education. It is clear that this argument could be skewed to conceptualise

---

[11] *The Catholic School on the Threshold of the Third Millennium*, 14.

[12] For a very insightful reflection on the role of memory in catechesis, see *Catechesi Tradendae*, 1979, 55.

[13] J.H. Newman, *An Essay on the Development of Christian Doctrine* (Notre Dame, Indiana: University of Notre Dame Press, 1878/2003), Chapter V. Newman identified seven 'notes' which ascertained the development of, as opposed to the corruption of, an idea. These seven notes are as follows; preservation of type; continuity of its principles; power of assimilation; logical sequence; anticipation of its future; conservative action upon its past; chronic vigour.

Religious Education as 'school-based catechesis' whereby the Shared Mission was, in practice, little more than a full-scale migration of the language and conceptual framework of faith development into syllabi of Religious Education. Magisterial teaching on (Catholic) school-based Religious Education, however, has moved away from this overtly *catechetical* approach towards a more nuanced vision designed to offer pupils a clear knowledge and understanding of Christianity and Christian life.[14]

Areas of Dissonance between Catechesis and Religious Education

Shared Mission is a way of bringing into harmony related but distinct concepts. Their distinctiveness is as important to the debate as their complementarity. Although catechesis is deemed a component part of broader faith development which includes but is not limited to school activity, it is important to clarify how the Catholic school can contribute towards specifically *catechetical* activity while avoiding an overly catechetical approach to Religious Education. To what extent is this possible? Nonetheless, this is an area of vital importance given the complex mix of confessional and cultural pluralism increasingly found in the contemporary Catholic school.[15]

The catechetical mission of the school is expressed in its wider life, especially in the availability of the sacraments, retreats and other apostolic initiatives. This broad and rich area of activity is clearly consonant with the idea that, owing to decline in opportunities for parish and family catechesis, the Catholic school might be the only site of genuine religious formation for young Catholics in contemporary society. Much more research is needed to assess how successful the Catholic school is as a site of religious formation when home/parish initiatives are lacking.

The subject of Religious Education draws on and is

---

[14] *Circular Letter to Presidents of Bishops' Conferences on Religious Education in Schools*, 2009, 17.

[15] J. Heft, *Catholic High Schools: Facing the New Realities*. (Oxford: Oxford University Press, 2011).

inspired by this deep-rooted faith tradition. Its contribution to the catechetical life of the Catholic school lies precisely in its educational credibility as a subject taught within a scholastic framework and promoting a synthesis of culture and life. The subject would boast of the same academic credentials as other subjects: visibility on school timetables; systematic planning of content according to recognized criteria; suitably qualified teachers; due consideration of appropriate methods of teaching and methods of assessment; the provision of suitable graded textbooks and other curricular resources; reporting of achievement to parents and other agencies and the motivation of pupils.[16]

The arrangement proposed above is a convincing expression of the relationship between *communio* and the Shared Mission. Catholic doctrine and a consonant worldview are experienced in the interrelated contexts of a catechetical setting and a scholastic setting. As this relationship is crucial to the success of the Catholic school, we now have to consider suitable ways of developing the Shared Mission.

---

[16] While Groome has argued (see above) that some form of academic rationale could be beneficially applied to catechetical programmes in parishes, a key difference seems to lie in the student audience and the intention of those who teach. The 'catechetical audience' gathers with a shared intention of developing faith. How strong this commitment to faith development is for younger children who, for example, have not elected to attend a First Communion programme outside of school hours, is a matter of debate. This caveat notwithstanding, there are still clear lines separating this audience from the generality of the pupils in a Catholic school who attend a Religious Education lesson.

CHAPTER 11
DEVELOPING THE SHARED MISSION

The relationship between catechesis and Religious Education can be summarised as follows: the aim of catechesis is faith-formation; the aim of Religious Education is knowledge of Christian doctrine and its relationship with wider culture. The latter is hence an *invitation* to, or a *deepening* of, faith but is cannot necessarily be configured according to catechetical concepts and language. In sum, faith-formation is its proximate, not its primary aim.

The relationship has been explored here in the context of the ecclesiological model of *communio*. The application of this particular theological/ecclesiological lens offers an original and granular perspective on the distinctive and fluid nature of the relationship between catechesis and Religious Education. It serves as a reminder that the frame of reference of Catholic Education, although rooted in the desire to offer a solid education to all, is best understood and appreciated by those keen to engage with the Church's theological vision.

Looking Back

Three claims were made at the start of the book. Here are some initial responses to the issues raised at the start of the journey.

1. *The relationship between Catechesis and Religious Education is most fully understood in broader historical and theological contexts.*

- Church teaching proposes a clear distinction between catechesis and Religious Education. This complementary and mutually-enriching distinction has both emerged from and fostered a wide body of relevant secondary literature.

- The study of these rich and varied historical contexts drew out the genealogy of the relationship between catechesis and Religious Education through four pivotal periods in the history of the Catholic Church. This genealogy exemplified the fluid nature of catechesis and the evolving relationship between Church thinking and broader events in society.

- The Magisterial documents on catechesis, education and Religious Education, while anchored in a fully Catholic theological vision, reflect a range of historical, educational and cultural contexts. This confirms the need for the Church to engage in dialogue with a wide body of opinion.

- Religious Education, as a term, is a recent arrival in the Catholic lexicon. It draws on catechesis but has a distinct educational flavour. While it can make a valid and worthy contribution to catechesis, its most appropriate conceptual framework is as a recognised curricular subject configured according to standard academic requirements.

2. *The theology of communio offers a suitable framework within which the partnership between catechesis and Religious Education can be understood.*

- The application of the theological lens of *communio* to the complex relationship between catechesis and Religious Education offers some clarity to both present and future discussions on the most suitable shape of the relationship.

- *Communio*, an ancient theological term, recovered in the early years of the twentieth-century, underpins the notion of the Church as a reflection of the Trinity (a communion of persons) and a place of encounter with Jesus Christ.

- *Communio* moves ecclesiology beyond the limitations of any 'political-society' model and encourages a deeper reflection on how the horizontal and vertical dimensions of the Church influence each other. At the heart of any reflection on *communio*-inspired studies is the need to appreciate unity-in-diversity and, of course, diversity-in-unity. The Church as an instrument of communion offers suitable opportunities for application in different parts of its life.

3. *Religious Education is a dynamic partnership between the principles of Catechesis and the principles of Catholic Education.*
  • The dialogic thread in *communio* can be usefully applied to the relationship between catechesis and Religious Education. A Spirituality of Communion, therefore, allows us to conceptualise catechesis and Religious Education as component parts of a Shared Mission.
  • Both catechesis and Religious Education contribute to an Integral *Religious* Formation emerging from the broader Integral *Human* Formation which lies at the heart of Catholic Education.
  • Catholic educators have the responsibility to develop a school syllabus which is theologically orthodox, pastorally sensitive and educationally strong;
  • In partnership with others, Catholic educators should ensure that Religious Education classes are not isolated from the wider life of the school. Religious Education should be part of a wider catechetical and cultural experience undertaken with parishes and other ecclesial bodies.

A Directory for Religious Education
  Despite the continual re-stating in the Magisterial documents of the distinctive yet complementary relationship between catechesis and Religious Education, there is still no suitable operational model for the subject. Catechists, for example, can draw on the principles laid out in the *General Directory for Catechesis* and, before that, the *General Catechetical Directory*: Catholic Religious Educators have no such universal template on which to draw.
  The field of Religious Education lacks, at present, a

dedicated document of similar status to the established catechetical directories of 1971 and 1997. The *Circular Letter* of 2009, as we have seen, aims simply to clarify the locus of Religious Education in the life of the school. Given the existence of a wide range of academic literature relating to developments in liberal Religious Education and the related fact that, unsurprisingly, much of this literature comes from outside the Catholic community, perhaps it is time to consider if a universal Directory of (Catholic) Religious Education would be beneficial to the Church's dedicated band of teachers. The breadth and depth of knowledge required in Religious Education both emerges from and contributes to an educational vision rooted in Catholic anthropology. Such an approach has implications for both content and pedagogy in the Catholic school's curriculum.

It is fair to ask how this Directory would look. What would its purpose be?

First, the proposed Directory would certainly draw on catechetical principles but set these within guidelines suitable for the vibrant and pluralist nature of contemporary Catholic schools. It would recognise that an overly catechetical approach could potentially weaken the academic status of school-based Religious Education while acknowledging that approaches too heavily influenced by theories of non-confessional Religious Education could dislocate it from the wider Catholic vision of education. The Directory would show how Religious Education has grown from distinct catechetical roots but it now has a different, although related, conceptual framework. It would be more than a differentiated version of the *General Directory for Catechesis*: its aim would be to enhance the academic standing of Religious Education within the Catholic community and beyond.

Second, the Directory would synthesise the various references to school-based Religious Education in existing Magisterial documents and set these in a wider academic and pastoral context. This would recognise the key influences of theology and catechesis while identifying the unique position of the Catholic school as a centre of Catholic culture.

Of course, the suggestion of a Directory could be interpreted as antithetical to the reality of a Spirituality of Communion. A document which attempts to harmonise the many manifestations of Religious Education across the world would be hard to achieve. Even if it were achievable, it could be unwelcome to those who would regard this as another mechanism designed to thwart local initiatives. More seriously, it would place at risk the key role of the local Bishop in determining the shape of Catholic Education and formation in his diocese.

Any possible tension between the universal and the local Church in this respect can be eased by close examination of the declared scope of both the *Catechism of the Catholic Church* and the *General Directory for Catechesis*. Both documents actively encourage local adaptations of their content while reminding all of the need to adhere to shared foundational principles. Any proposed Directory for Religious Education would be similarly constructed: it would present the key features of Catholic theology and its associated socio-cultural teachings in a systematic way and, crucially, outline the indicative content and associated pedagogy of a Religious Education syllabus. This would allow the Catholic school to remain firmly within the *communio* of the Church while serving as a place of meaningful dialogue/encounter with the teachings of the Catholic Church for those belonging to other theological and philosophical traditions.

There is much more to be done in this field. This study will serve as the conceptual basis for wider international studies of the ideal conceptual framework and underpinning principles of syllabi of Religious Education. Indeed, the territory of Religious Education, this unique interplay of theology, catechesis, educational philosophy and cultural studies, now needs to be re-proposed as the core of Catholic Education. I hope that this volume can be of assistance in this mission.

POSTSCRIPT

The Catholic school is called to retain and indeed celebrate a distinct *ecclesial* identity. That goes without saying. It must ensure that its educational vision is attractive and, indeed, open to those belonging to other religious and philosophical traditions. The Catholic school, as a civic as well as an ecclesial institution, is a key partner in dialogue on how best to shape *all* education systems and practices for the future.

There is a need for further exploration of how a properly-articulated distinction between catechesis and Religious Education can offer substantial theological, educational and pastoral capital for future debates on the place of religion/religious ways of thinking in public life. It is essential to find out how aware parish catechists and serving teachers are of the Magisterially-sanctioned distinction between wider catechesis and Religious Education in schools. Following on from this, we need to enquire how this affects, if at all, the manner in which they perform their duties and how they understand their respective role as catechists and teachers.

To move this debate forward, I propose four questions for further research:

Question 1: How can the Catholic school, while part of the *communio* of the Church, remain a civic institution where all are invited to explore the meaning of a 'good life' in a spirit of dialogue and freedom?

Question 2: What is the significance of the local educational context for the relationship between catechesis and Religious Education? For example, what role does the state play in the operation of Catholic Education and how does this inform the shape of the curriculum?

Question 3: How do syllabi of Religious Education, as configured by a range of local Churches and their educational agencies, reflect the Magisterial teaching on education?

Question 4: What is the relationship between programmes of Religious Education in the Catholic school and the various catechetical programmes – not just in sacramental preparation – offered to children who, for whatever reason, do not, or cannot, attend a Catholic school?

Addressing these questions at a local level would allow for extended research on the evolving nature of the relationship between catechesis and Religious Education across a variety of contexts.

There can be little doubt that Religious Education cannot operate successfully without a suitably coherent vision of education and schooling shaping other parts of the curriculum of the Catholic school. The presentation of inherited religious and cultural traditions must be a key component of the contemporary vision of Catholic Education in all its manifestations. This allows the Catholic school not just to remain faithful to its own mission but to stand as an example of good pedagogical practice to other models of schooling.

*   *   *   *   *

APPENDIX:
CATHOLIC EDUCATION: ITS NATURE, ITS DISTINCTIVENESS, ITS CHALLENGES[1]

I am grateful for the invitation to speak at the Launch of the St Andrew's Foundation as a new instrument in Scotland for the provision and support of Catholic Education and of Catholic teachers, and I wish, first of all, to acknowledge and celebrate the fruitful collaboration and partnership between the University of Glasgow and the Catholic Church in Scotland.

As a visitor from, and a representative of, the Holy See in Rome, it is heart-warming to be standing within the walls of an ancient University, whose degree awarding power still stands upon the Papal Bull of Pope Nicholas V, granted to establish the University in 1451.[2]

It is opportune at this present moment, amidst the rapidly changing state of society, of higher education generally and also of the Church, to reflect on the nature and distinctiveness of Catholic Education and on the challenges it

---

[1] Gerhard Cardinal Müller, Prefect of the Congregation for the Doctrine of the Faith, gave this lecture at the launch of the St Andrew's Foundation for Catholic Teacher Education, University of Glasgow, Scotland on 15 June 2013. This is an abridged version. The full text is available at http://www.gla.ac.uk/schools/education/standrewsfoundation/cardinalmullerslaunchaddress/

[2] Papal Bull of Pope Nicholas V, 7th January 1451: http://www.universitystory.gla.ac.uk/papal-bull/

both faces and also presents. The substance of my talk today will be to offer some thoughts and reflections on these important areas.

The Nature of Catholic Education

It is not insignificant to note that the vision and practice of Catholic Education has, throughout the Church's history, arisen out of a coming together of the Church with various cultures. The very mission of the Church, from its beginnings in the Upper Room in Jerusalem at Pentecost, has been to engage with the culture of the time and to seek to penetrate it with the message of the Gospel. At the same time, the Church has drawn on that culture and its wisdom, in order to help articulate her own self-understanding and to facilitate her own life and practice. From the beginning therefore, faith and culture have interacted, even when in certain periods of history, the interaction was more hostile and combative than collaborative.

It is not unknown to any of us that for many decades there have been voices raised against the idea of Catholic Education, against the fact of distinct faith schools and increasingly, in today's society, there are great challenges to the very idea of a religious education. Various charges are made which include the suggestion that religious education is a form of indoctrination and is contrary to the prevailing culture of freedom. Faith schooling is said to mitigate against social cohesion, encouraging intolerance, social prejudice, sectarianism and even bigotry. Within the Church herself, especially in the light of the call to the Church of recent Popes to the mission of New Evangelisation, there are voices which question the need for a separate Catholic Education. Should the Church not encourage a simple engagement with the wider society rather than maintain a separate system of education? Such are some of the questions that remain today as part of the melting pot of debates around educational issues. They will, no doubt, continue to be questions discussed and researched within this very Foundation in the coming years.

What it means to be Catholic

I would like to distinguish from the outset two important but different meanings of the word 'Catholic' within the debate about Catholic Education. In the first place, we may consider 'Catholic' to refer to a religious denomination, within society and the world at large, which is organised as a body of believers, who are admitted through baptism and whose membership can be described at the level of family, parish, diocese, the national Church and the international Church with her leadership in the Holy See in Rome. From this point of view Catholic Education is acknowledged by both Church and State as a fundamental right and primary responsibility of Catholic parents – the first educators of their children. In accordance with this fundamental right, the State has the duty and responsibility to facilitate the wishes of Catholic parents to educate their children according to their desire to pass on their faith to their children. Particular national states have sought to fulfil their responsibility in a variety of ways, enshrining within their systems of law different arrangements for this provision but always recognising the fundamental principle that those primarily responsible for the education of their children are their parents.

The Catholic Church also recognises the rights and duties of parents in the matter of education and from the earliest times has sought to provide support to parents, not least in the area of religious education. Within the rite of Baptism, in which parents seek the gift of faith for their children, parents also express their desire and their commitment "to raise their children in the practice of the Faith". The Church, for its part, has always regarded, as an essential element of its mission, the duty of providing the means for this. As John Henry Newman once wrote: For the Church "to baptise and not educate would be a grievous sin"!

The first justification therefore for the Church and State collaboration in the matter of Catholic Education is rooted in the universal and fundamental rights of parents.

This leads me to a second meaning of the word

'Catholic' which also has important implications for the Foundation whose launch we celebrate today. To illustrate my meaning, I would like to refer back to the great 5th century saint and classical exponent of Christian education Augustine of Hippo, who wrote a work called *The City of God*. The occasion of the composition was the accusation being made against Christians, that they were responsible for the fall of Rome. It was claimed that the beliefs, and more importantly, the practices, of Catholics were inimical to the Roman State and Roman society.

Augustine's response was to argue that far from undermining the State, Catholics practiced religious, moral and social virtues that precisely upheld the State. The reasons for the civil breakdown were to be found elsewhere – ultimately, within the very heart of man. *The City of God* is a comprehensive volume, which in many ways laid the foundations for dialogue between the civic state, the secular world and the Catholic Church – in Augustine's language, between the 'City of Man' and the 'City of God'. He argued that what was best in Roman society had its roots in Plato and Aristotle and great Roman minds, who had articulated the truth of the supreme Good, as the *telos* or 'End' of humanity – the Good that leads to happiness. They spoke of the good of the body, the good of the soul (of the mind and the will) and the good of the Common Weal (of Society).

At the heart of all of these goods was the development of the rational mind in conformity with the truth and the nourishing of the will through the attainment and practice of the virtues, of which Justice was seen as primary. The foundation was the human person, in whom they discovered a natural drive towards the discovery of the good and the true. We can recognise in Augustine's analysis the basis of much of the way that we speak even today about educational goals, especially in our concern for the whole person. Nevertheless, there was a problem. In the end, thought Augustine, this philosophy was not enough. Individuals and also society could never achieve the good to which they aspired. It is a perennial problem. The classical philosophy was groping towards an answer.

Augustine argued that Christians not only belong to the City of Man but also to the City of God. Embracing all that was true and good in the classical philosophy, belonging to the City of God brought in a number of new elements that both transformed and completed what was lacking in the classical philosophy and Roman society. In the first place, what is and can be known by the human mind is supplemented and completed by the truth of divine revelation. Like many of the great Christian minds in the early centuries, Augustine discovered in the Sacred Scriptures of the Old and New Testament the element that the classical philosophy, from which he himself came, was groping towards. God revealed himself in the history of the seemingly insignificant people of Israel and then most fully in the person of Jesus Christ.

Knowledge, which in classical philosophy was somewhat confined as a result of limitations within the reasoning human person, is both confirmed and completed. All reality and all truth, including the human person, have their source in the One God. In the history of Israel and in the person of Christ, God reveals his nature and also the ultimate nature and destiny of the human person – created by God in his own image and destined for eternal happiness, the ultimate good of humankind. The person of Jesus Christ is not only the fullness of God's self-revelation and the perfection of man, he is also the place of salvation, the place where the wounds in human nature are revealed and healed.

The ten commandments present as Moral Absolutes those goods that classical philosophy had perceived as the goods of the person and of society. But the Decalogue, and by implication, Greek and Roman philosophy, was in the end a pedagogy leading to Christ[3] who not only reveals the full meaning of the Commandments, but both accomplishes

---

[3] Cf. Gal 3:24-25

them in himself and provides the means of grace by which the very virtues of Christ become embodied in every other person. In Christ, said Augustine, the life of seeking the truth and living the virtues is realised, even though it means a slow progression with constant need of Christ's forgiveness and healing. Finally, for Augustine, the governing power in the City of God is a three-fold love – love of God, love of self and love of others. Love originates in the mystery of the Trinitarian relationships and is the motivation for Creation, Revelation and the Redemption in Christ. Within the City of God, love gathers, unifies and perfects all the human virtues.

If I can summarise Augustine's view of the key characteristics of the City of God, they are firstly faith – by which we have access to God and to the truth that he reveals in Christ; secondly hope, by which, in Christ, human weakness and sin is overcome and earthly goodness and blessedness is made possible and the mystery of eternal happiness becomes a true goal; and finally, love, which provides both the motivation for living and the goal of life without end. It is precisely, these three – faith, hope and love that are the gift of God, through Christ and the Holy Spirit in the Sacrament of Baptism. In the City of God, it is these three virtues that, in addition to the natural goods and virtues of the human person, are the heart of education.

We can see, therefore, that the word 'Catholic' has a fuller, more inclusive, sense. It implies an overarching philosophy of life, which includes, all that is good in the philosophies of societies and human culture. St Augustine contrasts citizenship in the City of Man with citizenship of the City of God. This is not a contrast between a worldly and an other-worldly approach, but concerns the breadth of one's philosophy of life and of education.

What it means to Educate

It is time now to turn more specifically to the second word in today's subject - Education. Few subjects are more contentious in today's society. Long gone are the days in which, in Christian Europe, there was a synthesis between Faith and Reason and a unity between the disciplines of various subjects in education, in which Theology was seen as the Queen of the Sciences. This was the atmosphere in which this University received its Papal Bull. It owed a great deal to the writings of the philosopher theologian – St Thomas Aquinas. Today there are a multitude of views about what education should be and how it should be carried out. There are views that emerge from Modernist and Post-Modern philosophies and ideologies; others emerge from State and political concerns, not least today because of the crisis in the economies of most European countries; and those from capitalist and market-driven theories and models. Finally, there is the overarching secular tone of society today with its emphasis on materialism and consumerism and the growing acceptance of a relativist stance with regard to truth and morality.

In his recent visit to Scotland and England, Pope Benedict XVI spoke of the serious danger of relativism which will undermine society and religion and in the end will be detrimental to the human person.[4] A proper understanding of education plays a significant part in providing an alternative to this relativist stance. From the time of Socrates education has been what the underlying Latin word suggests – a drawing out from the human person, through the training of the human mind, will and emotions, the ability to perceive and act upon the good and the true. The good and the true stand in some way outside the person, they are transcendent. The human person has a natural drive and curiosity to seek and understand them. A danger in the relativism of modern society is the assumption that human freedom essentially entails creating one's own truth and moral good. Notwithstanding the clear perception of the flaws within our nature, there are logical absurdities in the

---

[4] Pope Benedict XVI visited the United Kingdom in 2010.

relativists position: first – in asserting as absolutely true that there is no absolute truth; second – in maintaining that each person's truth is as valuable as another's; and third – in asserting that each person's morality is as good as the other's. The first represents the collapse of reason; the second and third, if pursued to their logical conclusion, would lead to the breakdown of society.

This is not to say that tolerance or human freedom are not values to be highly esteemed. The problem seems to be that such values are underpinned by a weak philosophy of life and of education, or at least one that is unarticulated or not critically examined. The result is the danger of trying to build society and to educate on the basis of weak foundations.

Here we touch upon one key element of the goals of higher education. It is surely part of the enterprise of higher education that it not simply mirror back the values of the society at large, nor simply that it produce those who will serve the economy through excellence in business or industry, science or the arts. An important element is also the ability to take a critical stance and examine the underlying assumptions, philosophies and ideologies in society today and especially those underlying the very disciplines that higher education pursues. There are those who will maintain that many of the disciplines are scientific and value-free. It is not difficult to refute such a claim. The bigger danger arises when the assumptions and philosophies are unexamined.

The St Andrew's Foundation can be a place for critical engagement with the philosophies that underpin the various ideas about education, not least within the University itself and also in the wider society, articulating a philosophy of life and understanding the nature of education found within the Catholic Church herself. This understanding is especially enshrined in the various documents concerning education that have emerged from the Holy See over the last century. I would like to take a moment to pay tribute to those who have published *An Anthology of Catholic Teaching on Education*, [editor, Leonard Franchi, Scepter, London, 2007] an excellent volume that brings together the significant Church documents, while indicating at the same time those which more particularly pertain to catechesis and those which pertain to Catholic Education more broadly. It would be hard to recommend a better resource for study within this new Foundation.

The Vision articulated by the Church

Both before the Second Vatican Council and since, the Church has consistently proclaimed the dignity of the human person, and the pattern and destiny for the person that is to be found in Christ. Education has a central place in the assertion of that dignity. In the first place, there are the important teachings of Popes Pius X and Pius XI. The particular challenge of their times concerned the extent and nature of the State's involvement in education. The Church had to struggle for her rights in the matter of teaching Christian doctrine in schools. Pope Pius XI's encyclical on Catholic Education, *Divini Illius Magistri* (1929), reflects the threat of the complete take-over of education by the State in a number of countries in which ideologies that deny or distort the dignity of the person, such as Communism, Fascism and Nazism were prevailing. In this hostile climate, Pope Pius XI clearly articulated an alternative vision, rooted in the basic rights of parents, explaining and defending the good of the human person as involving happiness and justice in this life, as well as the attainment of the person's ultimate and complete happiness in heaven. Happiness both in this life and definitively in heaven, was to be understood and pursued through the life of faith – the life communicated through a properly Catholic Education.

The period from the Second Vatican Council has seen, with the establishment of the Congregation for Catholic Education in Rome, the reaffirmation of the Church's teaching on the dignity of the human person and our destiny in Christ. The Council was expressly a time of returning to the Church's most ancient and secure sources; and of opening itself to the wider world. This was particularly focused on the Church's self-understanding and renewal and her salvific dialogue with the world. The Church looked afresh at the Scriptures and the Church Fathers in order to reflect on her own changing situation of being a missionary Church within an environment that was no longer a Christian culture. The Church needed to understand anew her own culture, with a history and a Tradition to transmit in a holistic way to her own future generations and to the world.

This process is ongoing and is a continued mining of the rich seams of Tradition. This is the underlying purpose of the Year of Faith that we are currently living in the Church. Pope Benedict's explicit invitation was to discover anew the documents of the Council and also the Council's primary fruit, the Catechism of the Catholic Church. The Catechism essentially represents a statement of Catholic culture expressed in the same structure as the New Testament statement of the culture of the early Church – "And they devoted themselves to the apostles' teaching and fellowship, to the breaking of bread and the prayers."[5]

This notion of the Church's culture implies also its transmission through education and leads to an engagement with the variety of cultures within which the Church finds herself today. The whole concept and project had its roots in the early Fathers of the Church who articulated, as I stated earlier in my discussion of Augustine's *City of God*, a vision of Catholic culture within the context of Greek and Roman society. Christian culture, and its transmission through education, was the Christianisation of the Greek concept of *Paideia* – a word that is difficult to translate but contains the idea of the holistic formation of the human person (body, mind and spirit), of the person *within* society and *within* civilisation or culture. In its baptised form, this process is envisaged as being under the pedagogy of God himself and directed towards a final civilisation within the mystery of the Trinity.

---

[5] Acts 2:42

It was in this same period both before and after the Council that the thought and writings of John Henry Newman were being more widely disseminated especially with regard to his teaching on Conscience and on Education. Newman himself was deeply influenced by the traditions of the Fathers, and the notion of *Paideia* stood behind much of his educational thought. It is not insignificant that the occasion of the recent Papal visit of Pope Benedict was also the time that Newman was beatified. At that time Pope Benedict said of him:

I would like to pay particular tribute to his vision for education, which has done so much to shape the ethos that is the driving force behind Catholic schools and colleges today. Firmly opposed to any reductive or utilitarian approach, he sought to achieve an educational environment in which intellectual training, moral discipline and religious commitment would come together. The project to found a Catholic University in Ireland provided him with an opportunity to develop his ideas on the subject, and the collection of discourses that he published as *The Idea of a University* holds up an ideal from which all those engaged in academic formation can continue to learn.

The Nature of the Church as Mystery, Communion and Mission

The reflection initiated at the Second Vatican Council on Catholic culture and its transmission has found articulation, not only in the Constitutions of the Second Vatican Council, and in the Catechism, but also in the structure of the Church as Mystery, Communion and Mission. And its particular application to Catholic Education was enshrined in the most recent document from the Congregation for Catholic Education entitled *Educating Together in Catholic Schools*, published in the same year (2007) as the *Anthology*.

It is important to understand what the idea of the Church as Mystery, Communion and Mission involves. Fundamental is Communion – which is another way of expressing Catholic culture and its central affirmation of human dignity as bearing the pattern and the destiny of Christ. Communion comes about through initial conversion to the person of Christ and necessarily leads to communion with everything with which Christ is in communion. In other words, it leads to communion with His Body, the Church, with her life and sacraments, her teaching and with each and every person who makes up the Church. Communion with Christ also opens up to us all, as both its origin and its goal, entry into the Mystery of the life of the Blessed Trinity. And communion within the Body of Christ and communion with the persons of the Trinity give rise to the Mission of the Church to draw all of humanity into this life and culture. Indeed, this is ultimately the mission of the Trinity itself – to draw every created person, through the Church, into participation in the Trinitarian life.

It is in this vision of a truly Catholic culture that the most recent document, to which I have referred, *Educating Together in Catholic Schools,* discusses the nature and purpose of education and in particular, the joint activity of lay and consecrated persons within the field of education. The document presents a new and challenging statement both of the human person and of the purpose of education. This new statement is set in the language of Communion.

Every human person is called to communion because of his nature which is created in the image and likeness of God.[6] Therefore, within the sphere of biblical anthropology, man is not an isolated individual, but a person, a being who is essentially relational. The communion to which man is called always involves a double dimension, that is to say vertical (communion with God) and horizontal (communion with people). It is fundamental that communion be acknowledged as a gift of God, as the fruit of the divine initiative fulfilled in the Easter mystery .

This description of the human person is inspired by the Church's understanding and vision of what it is to be a human being and as a response to the present cultural

---

6 Gen 1:26-27

context. Young people are growing up in a world marked by moral relativism, individualism, utilitarianism and a lack of interest in the fundamental truths of human life. The Church is almost alone, it seems, in being prepared to assert the dignity the human person as bearing the image of God - a vision available to reason, and once deep at the heart of western culture, but which is now so generally denied. It is when humans are no longer seen to bear the image of God, that human freedom is reduced to mere arbitrary whim, and the pursuit of true value is reduced to a consumerism that never satisfies. The Church must give back to young people the true understanding of their own value that has been taken from them. And this requires the communication of the Catholic faith concerning our true destiny in Christ. This re-proclamation and defence of humanity and its true worth lies at the centre of the Church's Mission - her calling of all people to their true destiny in Christ. We are duty bound to use every possible opportunity to articulate this vision and form future generations in it.

In the midst of so many diverse and at times bewildering versions of educational aims and processes, the Church has a rich and vital vision to proclaim. At its heart is an ideal of the person as called to love and friendship - with God and with fellow humans as bearing his image. Catholic Education is an expression of a Catholic culture that is ever drawing upon the richness of its Tradition and the cultures of the ages, ever seeking to renew and re-state itself, and always conscious that it does so within the pedagogical mission of God himself in the world. It is a vision that needs to be heard in the world as the Church seeks to serve the world that God loves. As well as seeking to dialogue with today's society, the Church also seeks to live out and incarnate in every place the vision that by God's grace she articulates. May this new Institute play an important role in the study of this vision, its dissemination for the formation of Catholic teachers, and support of the schools in which this vision becomes realised.

PRE-PUBLICATION REVIEWS

This volume on the relationship between catechesis and Religious Education is a timely reminder of the importance of authentic Catholic Education. As the Church of the New Evangelisation, we need increasingly to deepen our engagement with the many traditions and practices revealed in Sacred Tradition. Catholic Religious Education should help us to do this.

Our Catholic educational heritage is a gift to humanity, not just a private tradition to be cherished by the baptised. Catholic Education must have a commitment to the formation of the baptised. The Religious Education curriculum contributes to the faith formation of the baptised by presenting the Sacred Tradition in an accessible and systematic way.

Communion comes about through initial conversion to the person of Christ and necessarily leads to communion with everything with which Christ is in communion.

This is the task that lies ahead. I ask all with an interest in the Catholic educational project to consider seriously the issues raised in this important volume.

Gerhard Cardinal Müller
Prefect, Congregation for the Doctrine of the Faith

* * * * *

This is an important book, concise and tightly argued, that addresses a perennial issue in Catholic education, the relationship between religious education and catechesis. Franchi offers a new perspective by proposing a more theological understanding be used in framing the debate. He argues for seeing the relationship within an ecclesiological understanding of the Church as *communio*. On this basis a shared mission can be best realized, one that is faithful to the broader vision of Catholic education as well as being responsive to particular cultural circumstances.

A feature of the book is the integration of a strong historical perspective and magisterial documents on education. This book makes an invaluable contribution to the ongoing discussion on the future of religious education in Catholic schools.

Professor Richard Rymarz
Head of Religious Education and Director of Research
Broken Bay Institute, Pennant Hills, NSW 2120 Australia